Echoes of the Gospel in Harry Potter

Echoes of the Gospel in Harry Potter

CLAY MYATT

WIPF & STOCK · Eugene, Oregon

ECHOES OF THE GOSPEL IN HARRY POTTER

Wipf & Stock
An Imprint of Wipf and Stock Publishers
199 W. 8th Ave., Suite 3
Eugene, OR 97401

www.wipfandstock.com

PAPERBACK ISBN: 978-1-6667-0868-4
HARDCOVER ISBN: 978-1-6667-0869-1
EBOOK ISBN: 978-1-6667-0870-7

AUGUST 26, 2021

To Caleb, Tawney, and Tara,
who share my love of Harry Potter

No story has power, nor will it last, unless we feel in ourselves that it is true, and true of us.

—JOHN STEINBECK, *EAST OF EDEN*

Contents

Acknowledgments

THERE ARE A NUMBER of people I would like to thank who helped make this book a reality. First, I would like to thank those who read parts of the book ahead of time and shared their thoughts: Sean Cawley, Blake Banks, Matt Girgis, Natalie Van Hoose, Mike Roop, Lily Dykes, Ali Haq, and Caleb Myatt. I would also like to especially thank Ben Lowe and Brant Bonetti for the more detailed editing they did on a number of the chapters. Additionally, I am very grateful to the insights that both Sarah Wears-Garcia and Jennifer Guo gave me on the publishing world. And finally, I want to thank Wipf and Stock Publishers for taking on this project from a first-time author. It is much appreciated.

Of course, a book does not get written overnight, and thus I would like to thank some of the many people who have shaped and supported me up to this point in my life. First, my family: Mom, Dad, Caleb, Tawney, and Tara. Thank you for your support and encouragement throughout the various seasons of my life. And to my high school friends—Alex, Dan, Kyle, Malcolm, Matt, Nick, and Teja—I am very grateful for our ongoing friendships and enjoy every chance we get to hang out.

Second, I would like to thank the friends and mentors who have walked with me, lamented with me, and encouraged me through the past five years of my life as I have dealt with health issues. There are a number of people I could list here, but I would especially like to thank Sean Cawley, Josh Jeans, Brant Bonetti, Matt Girgis, Henry Thompson, Caleb Valentine, Blake Banks, Ben

Lowe, Jonathan Sites, Rick Eimers, and Josh Stone. Whether it was conversations, phone calls, prayers, or simply hanging out, you all have helped me to persevere and pursue the things God has called me to. Chapter 7 of this book is about the friendship between Harry, Ron, and Hermione, and I dedicate that chapter to you all for giving me a taste of what this friendship is like.

Third, I want to thank a few of the churches that have particularly shaped and formed me. First, Cuyahoga Valley Church, the church I grew up in. Thank you for giving me my first exposure to what a church seeking to follow Jesus should look like. And thank you in particular to Rick Duncan for giving me the opportunity to serve as an intern when I was in college and for mentoring me in my call to pastoral ministry. Second, I want to thank Creekside Community Church. You all are where I learned what it means to be a pastor, so thank you to the pastors who taught me so much (Steve Gregg, Mike Roop, Steve Lammers, and Mitch Cruit) and to the entire church family for being a warm and loving community. A special thank-you to my wonderful One Another Group there. And lastly, I want to thank Trinity Baptist Church for your support and encouragement throughout the year I served as assistant pastor.

Finally, in a book about Harry Potter, I think it is fitting for me to acknowledge the impact of J. K. Rowling on my life. As I have been writing this book and reflecting on the Harry Potter series, I have marveled at the fact that Rowling started writing this series when she was just twenty-five years old. As I think will become clear, it took more than just great writing skill to compose this series; it also took deep wisdom and insight, and I think it is a testament to who she is as a person. I hope people will enjoy and benefit from her work, as I have, for years to come.

Introduction

My first time reading through the Harry Potter series was in the summer of 2017, exactly twenty years after *Harry Potter and the Sorcerer's Stone* was first published. I had an eight-hour drive ahead of me, and so, given the fact that almost everyone I knew had read the books, I decided to give the first book a listen as I drove. I was immediately hooked. Over the rest of that summer, I finished all seven books, and I believed then, as I do now, that I had just read one of the greatest stories ever written. The magical world was fascinating and captured my imagination. The characters were highly memorable yet relatable. And the plotline was unpredictable yet satisfyingly fitting. Here I was, at twenty-four years old, being deeply moved by a story that was initially intended for children—a fact which, I think, speaks volumes about how deep and profound this story really is.

As a Christian pastor, I have read the Bible a number of times, and my favorite book has always been the Gospel of John. On the surface, the Gospel of John is quite simple and can be adequately understood by most people. But standing behind this simplicity is an ocean of meaning such that one can read it over and over again and still discover new insights. It is shallow enough that a child may wade yet deep enough that an elephant may swim.[1] I think Harry Potter is similar. The story is simple enough that children can read it and love it, yet it also has such depth that adults will re-read it again and again because new insights come with each reading. Perhaps this multi-level appeal is why over 500 million copies of Harry Potter have been sold, making it by far the best-selling book series of all time.[2]

In an essay called "On Fairy-Stories," J. R. R. Tolkien (the author of *The Lord of the Rings*) described the essence of fairy tales and why people love reading them. Three things, he said, draw us to fairy tales: Recovery, Escape, and Consolation. He defines Recovery as the "regaining of a clear view"—that is, "seeing things as we are . . . meant to see them."[3] Perhaps paradoxically, Tolkien is saying that fairy tales clarify our perspective on real life. Escape is a broader category that includes escaping time, conversing with non-human creatures, escaping from pain and sorrow, and ultimately escaping death—desires, he says, which we all have and which are fulfilled in part through reading fairy tales.[4] And Consolation is "the joy of the happy ending: or more correctly of the good catastrophe, the sudden joyous 'turn' (for there is no true end to any fairy-tale)."[5] In the face of the sadness and despair that we often find in our midst, the joy we taste in a fairy tale's euphoric resolution (what Tolkien calls the "eucatastrophe") is like a breath of fresh air.

Tolkien ends his essay, however, quite boldly—he claims that the greatest of all fairy tales has actually happened in history:

> The Gospels contain a fairy-story, or a story of a larger kind which embraces all the essence of fairy-stories. They contain many marvels . . . and among the marvels is the greatest and most complete conceivable eucatastrophe. But this story has entered History and the primary world. . . . The Birth of Christ is the eucatastrophe of Man's history. The Resurrection is the eucatastrophe of the story of the Incarnation. This story begins and ends in joy. . . . There is no tale ever told that men would rather find was true, and none which so many sceptical men have accepted as true on its own merits.[6]

In other words, the gospel—the story the Bible is telling that climaxes in Jesus Christ—is the greatest of all fairy tales, and incredibly, this fairy tale has come true.

If Tolkien is right, then we should expect to find echoes of the gospel in every fairy tale. That is why I have named this book *Echoes of the Gospel in Harry Potter*. I borrowed the title from

Richard Hays, a Bible scholar from Duke University, who wrote *Echoes of Scripture in the Gospels* and *Echoes of Scripture in the Letters of Paul* to show how the New Testament writers were echoing the Old Testament in their writings. Of course, there is a key difference between Hays's books and my own: the writers of the New Testament saw themselves as continuing the story that had begun in the Old Testament, which J. K. Rowling is obviously not attempting to do in Harry Potter. Nevertheless, there are two explicit quotations from the Bible in Harry Potter,[7] and Rowling herself acknowledges the influence of the biblical story line on her work: "To me, the religious parallels have always been obvious. . . . But I never wanted to talk too openly about it because I thought it might show people who just wanted the story where we were going."[8]

The purpose of this book is to tease out some of those parallels. I do not think there has ever been another story that more closely resembles the biblical story line than Harry Potter, and I believe that it is these parallels that have made this the best-selling story of all time. It has the clearest links to the greatest of all fairy tales. This will be quite a different approach, then, from that of people who thought the Harry Potter books were dangerous and a threat to Christianity when they were first published. I think this initial pushback the books got from some Christians is part of the reason why there has been so little Christian reflection on them, particularly in comparison to series like *The Lord of the Rings* and The Chronicles of Narnia.

There are three kinds of people who I hope will read this book. First, I hope that if you are a Christian, you will read this book and grow in your appreciation of the gospel. Those of us who have been Christians for a while can sometimes forget how wonderful this story is. I have found that one of the effects of reading a story like Harry Potter is that it can help us see the beauty of the gospel from new angles and remind us how extraordinary it is that this story has come true in Jesus. Furthermore, many who grew up reading Harry Potter now have children themselves and are reading the books with their children. I hope those parents will find this book to be helpful in pointing out some of the many ways that the Harry Potter series echoes the gospel so that they can talk about these things with their children.

Second, I also hope that you will read this book if you are not a Christian but have read Harry Potter and share my enjoyment of the story. You may be unconvinced by Tolkien's assertion that the story of Jesus Christ—this greatest of fairy tales—has come true. My hope is that as the parallels between Harry Potter and the biblical story line are made, you will see what Tolkien saw—namely that the gospel has the "inner consistency of reality."[9] You might just find that what you love about Harry Potter is an echo of the gospel.

And third, perhaps surprisingly, I hope that if you are hurting, you will read this book and be encouraged by it. My introduction to Harry Potter has come at a very difficult season in my life, which I think is partly why this story has been so meaningful to me. Since the spring of 2016, I have dealt with debilitating health issues that have left me with chronic pain and have kept me from doing things I love, like running and playing sports. Having this part of my life taken away from me has been very hard to cope with. During this time, other challenges related to relationships and career have swirled together with the chronic pain into a perfect storm of disappointment, discouragement, and, at times, despair. It is while facing these hardships that I first read Harry Potter, and I have found the series' portrayal of pain and suffering refreshing.

Contrary to the prevailing narratives in our culture that tend to view suffering as only something to be avoided or fixed, the message of Harry Potter is that suffering can be meaningful, that it can make one more loving and courageous, that it can even create the circumstances out of which heroism arises, and that it will ultimately end. I have been encouraged to keep pressing on in my pain and suffering as a result of reading this story, and I want to share my insights with others. Writing this book has been a way for me to find healing myself, and my hope and prayer is that these would be words of healing for others as they lay out the hope of the gospel.

In each chapter, you will find a discussion of a major concept, character, or theme in Harry Potter along with how that concept, character, or theme echoes a part of the gospel. My list is certainly not exhaustive, but since cuts had to be made somewhere, I chose the moments that were most moving and meaningful to me. In a sense, the order in which you read these chapters does not matter, although I did consider the story line of Harry Potter when ordering the chapters. If you do read them in order, you will more naturally follow the story line of the series. I hope you enjoy.

PART I

The Magical World

1

The Prophecy

To Harry Potter—the boy who lived!

—Witches and Wizards all over England[10]

In the opening chapter of *Harry Potter and the Sorcerer's Stone*, we are introduced not to Harry, but to the aggressively normal members of the Dursley family. The Dursleys are trying to navigate an average day, but their pursuit of ordinariness is repeatedly hindered by strange occurrences and strange figures who insist on celebrating some unknown event. These figures, who turn out to be witches and wizards, are so rambunctious in their festivities because, as Dumbledore says, they have had "precious little to celebrate for eleven years."[11] The wizarding world has been in a state of darkness and despair because of the evil perpetrated by Lord Voldemort and his followers. And things are looking bleak. The Death Eaters outnumber those resisting them twenty-to-one, and there are disappearances and deaths all the time. People are living in a state of anxious fear with very little hope of victory.

And then, all of a sudden, Lord Voldemort is vanquished . . . by a baby boy of all people! It is like the sun shining through a break in the clouds after a long, dark storm, and people finally have a reason to rejoice and be happy again. This is an event worth celebrating! No wonder witches and wizards break out in feasts and parties and set off shooting stars.

The story is very reminiscent of some of the events surrounding the birth of another baby boy two thousand years ago: Jesus of Nazareth. The context of this boy's birth was also one of darkness and despair: The people of Israel had been exiled from their homeland due to their rejection of God and his ways. And even though they had returned some years later, they still felt enslaved in their land, and things had never quite been the same. Since that time, they had been ruled by a number of different cruel and oppressive regimes, the latest being the Roman Empire. Israel was expecting God to come to his people and deliver them from such powers, but they had been waiting for centuries, and the waiting was hard and wearying.

And then, all of a sudden it seems, a series of different people begin to have odd dreams and visions. An angel appears to an old priest who is married to a barren woman, and he is told that his wife will give birth to a great prophet who will call the Jews to return to their God (Luke 1:5–25). And more significantly, the same angel appears to a virgin girl and tells her that she will give birth to a son who will reign over a kingdom that will never end (Luke 1:26–38). His name is to be Jesus, and he is the Messiah, the promised king who will rescue the Jews from captivity and rule with justice and righteousness. He is the one who will vanquish evil for good.

And the people finally have reason to rejoice again, because Jesus is the light who has come "to shine on those living in darkness and in the shadow of death" (Luke 1:79). As Tolkien says, the birth of the Messiah is the "eucatastrophe"—the shocking but glorious turn—of humanity's history.[12] After the long, dark night of oppressive rulers, the sun is finally starting to rise. God has come to rescue his people. This is good news of great joy worth celebrating! No wonder a great company of angels breaks out into song: "Glory to God in the highest heavens, and on earth peace to those on whom his favor rests" (Luke 2:14).

But there are two other significant similarities between baby Harry vanquishing Lord Voldemort and the birth of Jesus of Nazareth. First, both events were prophesied. Before Harry was born, Sybill Trelawney, the future Divination professor at Hogwarts, made a prophecy to Dumbledore during her job interview in the Hog's Head. It said that a child would be born at the end of July who would have the power to defeat the Dark Lord. And then the crucial line: "The Dark Lord will mark him as his equal, but he will have power the Dark Lord knows not."[13]

Voldemort was never told this second half of the prophecy, though, because Snape, the eavesdropper, only heard the first half before getting caught. Therefore, Voldemort, believing Harry to be the child of the prophecy, made plans to kill him. But by setting out to kill Harry, Voldemort unknowingly marked him as his equal and gave him great power, thus fulfilling the prophecy. And it was this power that Voldemort gave Harry that would wind up being his downfall. As Dumbledore later says, "[Voldemort] not only handpicked the man most likely to finish him, he handed him uniquely deadly weapons!"[14]

The birth of Jesus was also prophesied. Indeed, after his resurrection, Jesus said, "Everything must be fulfilled that is written about me in the Law of Moses, the Prophets and the Psalms" (Luke 24:44). In other words, Jesus was claiming that the whole Old Testament spoke about his coming. Entire books have been written on this subject, which cannot be addressed here, but I will mention one specific prophecy: the one that came first. This prophecy was given in a moment of great pain—just after the first humans, Adam and Eve, disobeyed God in the garden of Eden. Their rebellion brought a great curse upon the world that left no part untouched. Humans were broken. Their relationships with each other were broken. And the rest of creation was broken.

But God made a promise. Adam and Eve had been tempted by a serpent, a crafty and deceitful creature whom we later learn is Satan, the archenemy of God and his people (Revelation 12:9). And to that serpent, God said, "I will put enmity between you and the woman, and between your offspring and hers; he will crush your head, and you will strike his heel" (Genesis 3:15). Thousands of years later, Jesus came as the woman's offspring and fulfilled this prophecy; he is the one who ultimately crushed the head of the serpent. But the shocking thing about this is that the way Jesus defeated Satan is through dying (see Hebrews 2:14–18). It is through letting the serpent strike his heel, as it were, that he crushes the head of the serpent.

And, apparently, Satan did not know this would happen. In fact, Satan is the one who initiates the sequence of events that leads to the crucifixion of Jesus by entering Judas, one of Jesus' disciples, and instigating him to betray Jesus and hand him over to the religious leaders (Luke 22:3). As the apostle Paul later wrote, if "the rulers of this age" (Satan being the chief of them) had understood the wisdom of God in the crucifixion of Jesus, "they would not have crucified the Lord of glory" (1 Corinthians 2:8). They would not have brought about their own demise. And so just as Voldemort's attack on baby Harry led to his downfall, so it is through striking Jesus that Satan ultimately meets his downfall.

The other similarity between these two stories about babies is the scope of who is affected by them. As Mr. Dursley is leaving work on the day Lord Voldemort disappears, he accidentally bumps into an old wizard and almost knocks him over. Instead of being irritated by this, though, the wizard gives Mr. Dursley a hug and says, "Nothing could upset me today! Rejoice, for You-Know-Who has gone at last! Even Muggles like yourselves should be celebrating, this happy, happy day!"[15] The point is that even though Voldemort is a wizard and wreaked havoc in the wizarding world, his evil affected Muggles as well. They also experienced death and destruction because of his terrorism, and therefore they should be rejoicing that he is gone.

The same is true of Jesus. Jesus is the Jewish Messiah, who came to deliver his people from their enemies (Luke 1:54–55). And he did do that. But the scope of his mission is so much larger. He came not just to be a light for Jews living in darkness; he came to be "a light for revelation to the Gentiles [non-Jews]" (Luke 2:32). He is the Savior of the entire world—including those of us who are not Jewish (John 4:42)! Indeed, his mission is so cosmic in scope that its final goal is that "the earth will be filled with the knowledge of the LORD as the waters cover the sea" (Isaiah 11:9). The whole world will be flooded with God's healing presence and restored. This is why not just Jewish shepherds but also Gentile Magi from the east come to Bethlehem to worship baby Jesus. Even Gentiles celebrated this happy day because the birth of King Jesus was good news for them as well.

2

Magic

Harry—yer a wizard.

—RUBEUS HAGRID[16]

THE MAIN CHARACTERISTIC THAT sets the wizarding world apart from our own is the presence of magic. It is the foundation upon which Harry Potter is built, and it is what inspires so many people to read and enjoy the story. A good summary of what is so appealing about magic comes from Horace Slughorn when he describes the effects of Felix Felicis to his Potions students, one of whom will receive a vial of this potion as a prize. He warns them that Felix Felicis is prohibited in competitions, so "the winner is to use it on an ordinary day only . . . and watch how that ordinary day becomes extraordinary!"[17] Felix Felicis makes the ordinary extraordinary—which is exactly what magic does. It enchants the world by taking ordinary things in our world and making them extraordinary.

This happens in all sorts of ways. And because Harry was raised by his aunt and uncle away from the magical world, as readers we are immersed in the magical world for the first time just as he is. First, of course, there is Hogwarts School of Witchcraft and Wizardry. For many kids, school is mundane and boring, but Hogwarts could not be more different! For starters, it is a majestic castle in the mountains overlooking a lake—one would be hard-pressed to find a more beautiful place to live and learn. But it is the magic of the castle that is especially remarkable. Food appears on the table from the kitchens downstairs. The ceiling of the Great Hall is enchanted to look like the sky, giving students the sensation of being outside even when they are inside. The statues and portraits can move and talk. Ghosts (and Peeves) float through the rooms and corridors keeping students on their toes. First years are sorted into houses by the Sorting Hat based on certain traits they possess to help facilitate friendships and keep students from feeling isolated when they arrive. And of course, students are taught Charms and Defense Against the Dark Arts instead of English and Physics. Simply put, most children would find going to school at Hogwarts far more exciting than ordinary school.

Houses in the magical world are similarly extraordinary. Harry's first time in a wizarding family's home is in the second book when he visits the Burrow, the home of the Weasleys. Here, he witnesses how magic makes housework less tedious. Knives can cut food by themselves. Dishes can wash themselves. Tables and chairs can be set up with the wave of a wand. Mrs. Weasley also has a clock on her kitchen wall with a hand for each member of her family pointing to things like "work," "school," and "traveling," thus alleviating some of the maternal anxiety of not knowing where your children are.[18] Furthermore, homeowners in the wizarding world fight infestations not just of weeds and dust, but also of garden gnomes and doxies—certainly a greater challenge but also a welcome change from the drudgery of house chores.

Transportation is also enhanced by magic. One of the frustrations of moving from one place to another is that it can take a lot of time and be delayed by unforeseen circumstances. Magic mitigates these hindrances. There are many ways that one can travel in the wizarding world, some of which involve flying—such as by broomsticks, flying animals, and flying cars—and some of which are even more efficient—such as Floo powder, Portkey, and Apparition. But regardless of mode, they all avoid the frustration of traffic and delays, and they sound a lot more fun.

Medicine likewise looks very different in the magical world. There is a humorous exchange between Ron and Harry while they are at St. Mungo's visiting Mr. Weasley that demonstrates this well. Harry sees witches and wizards in lime-green robes, and he asks Ron if they are doctors. Ron responds, "Doctors? Those Muggle nutters that cut people up? Nah, they're Healers."[19] Of course, doctors do more than just cut people up and they do facilitate healing, but many times there is nothing they can do for our problems. And it is in those moments that we wish they were Healers. We wish that our injuries and illnesses could be taken away with the wave of a wand, and many of them can in Harry Potter.

Magic enchants many other aspects of life as well: banking (Gringotts), work (the Ministry of Magic), celebrations and holidays (Hogwarts feasts), sports (Quidditch), time (the Time-Turner), and memory (the Pensieve), to name a few. But the other fascinating part of life that magic affects is the relationships formed between humans and nonhumans. In our world, we have the ability to tame and give commands to animals, but in Harry Potter real relationships are formed between humans and animals. Owls can be told with precise detail where to take letters. Cats like Crookshanks have the ability to help humans by recognizing deception. Snakes can be conversed with if the witch or wizard has the ability to speak Parseltongue. Creatures like Hippogriffs and Thestrals can be flown. Phoenixes can come to the aid of their owners in crucial moments of need. Moreover, there are other nonhuman magical creatures that witches and wizards can speak to as if they were humans, such as house-elves, centaurs, goblins, giants, and merpeople. In his essay "On Fairy-Stories," Tolkien says that the ability to converse with nonhuman creatures is one of the reasons we read fairy tales, and I think it is certainly one of the magical elements of the wizarding world that draws people to Harry Potter.[20]

I have said that the beauty of magic is that, like Felix Felicis, it takes the ordinary, frustrating parts of our world and makes them extraordinary. But the Bible teaches that the world was not always so frustrating. It teaches that once upon a time people lived in harmony with one another, with God, and with the world around them. But then the first humans disobeyed God, and they brought a terrible curse upon themselves and upon the world. God said to them:

> Cursed is the ground because of you;
>   through painful toil you will eat food from it
>   all the days of your life.
> It will produce thorns and thistles for you,
>   and you will eat the plants of the field.
> By the sweat of your brow
>   you will eat your food
> until you return to the ground,
>   since from it you were taken;
> for dust you are
>   and to dust you will return. (Genesis 3:17–19)

Part of the curse for humanity's disobedience is that when they try to grow food, it produces thorns and thistles for them. Their work has become toilsome and painful. And these "thorns and thistles" have infiltrated every aspect of our world. The apostle Paul says that the "*whole* creation has been groaning as in the pains of childbirth right up to the present time" (Romans 8:22). Every good part of our lives is infested to some degree by the curse of these thorns and thistles.

The beauty of magic in Harry Potter, though, is that it takes a stab at reversing the curse. The frustrations of school, home, transportation, medicine, work, and so many other parts of life are lessened in the magical world. And we get a taste of what pre-curse life might be like.

But the Bible teaches that one day the curse will actually be reversed. It says, "Christ redeemed us from the curse of the law by becoming a curse for us—for it is written, 'Cursed is everyone who is hanged on a tree'" (Galatians 3:13 ESV). Because Jesus Christ was crucified and hung on a wooden cross (a tree), he took the curse of humanity's disobedience on himself so that it would be exhausted and no longer have a hold on us. And because he did that, the day is coming when all the effects of the curse will be gone. The prophet Isaiah describes what God will do like this:

See, I will create
  new heavens and a new earth.
The former things will not be remembered,
  nor will they come to mind.
But be glad and rejoice forever
  in what I will create,
for I will create Jerusalem to be a delight
  and its people a joy.
I will rejoice over Jerusalem
  and take delight in my people;
the sound of weeping and of crying
  will be heard in it no more.

Never again will there be in it
  an infant who lives but a few days,
  or an old man who does not live out his years;
the one who dies at a hundred
  will be thought a mere child;
the one who fails to reach a hundred
  will be considered accursed.
They will build houses and dwell in them;
  they will plant vineyards and eat their fruit.
No longer will they build houses and others live in them,
  or plant and others eat.
For as the days of a tree,
  so will be the days of my people;
my chosen ones will long enjoy
  the work of their hands.
They will not labor in vain,
  nor will they bear children doomed to misfortune;
for they will be a people blessed by the LORD,
  they and their descendants with them.
Before they call I will answer;
  while they are still speaking I will hear.
The wolf and the lamb will feed together,
  and the lion will eat straw like the ox,
  and dust will be the serpent's food.
They will neither harm nor destroy
  on all my holy mountain,
says the LORD. (Isaiah 65:17–25)

This vision is a world in which people's work is no longer frustrating and toilsome. A world in which they no longer die of disease. A world in which all struggle and pain have ceased. And a world in which humans live in harmony and restored fellowship with animals. In short, this is a world where ordinary life has become extraordinary.

In light of this, the invitation to us is to join God in this work he is doing. Yes, we still feel the effects of the curse, but those who believe in Jesus are already part of the new creation: "The old has gone, the new is here" (2 Corinthians 5:17)! And God does not just make us into new creations for the sake of it; he transforms us so that we can be agents in his work of "making all things new" (Revelation 21:5 ESV). Thus, the proper response to hearing that God is restoring the world is not to sit and watch—it is to join in the "magic" and, filled with the Holy Spirit, to work towards the renewal of this world, of which it will one day be said, "No longer will there be any curse" (Revelation 22:3).

3

The Mirror of Erised

*So . . . you, like hundreds before you, have discovered
the delights of the Mirror of Erised.*

—ALBUS DUMBLEDORE[21]

ONE OF THE MOST mysterious magical objects in the wizarding
world is the Mirror of Erised. A colossal and beautiful mirror, it
has an unintelligible inscription on it that adds to its mystique:
"Erised stra ehru oy tube cafru oyt on wohsi."[22] However, when
the inscription is read backwards, it says, "I show not your face
but your heart's desire." This is the magic of the Mirror: instead of
revealing a person's face or appearance, like most mirrors do, the
Mirror of Erised reveals what is inside of us. Or as Dumbledore
says, "It shows us nothing more or less than the deepest, most desperate desire of our hearts."[23]

As such, everybody sees something different when they
look into the Mirror. Harry sees his parents because he has never
known them. Ron sees himself winning awards such as Head Boy
and holding the House Cup and the Quidditch Cup because he
has been overshadowed by the success of his five brothers. Quirrell
sees himself presenting the Sorcerer's Stone to Voldemort because
he wants to please his master. And this is where the genius of the
Mirror lies: Dumbledore hides the Sorcerer's Stone in the Mirror

so that only the person who wants to take the Stone, but not use it, will be able to look into the Mirror and find it. Otherwise, the person will look into the Mirror and only see what they want to use the Stone for. This is why Harry is able to find the Stone—he was not intending to use it to extend his life or make gold.

Though the Mirror of Erised plays a prominent role in the first book, it is also alluded to later in the series. When Harry asked Dumbledore what he saw in the Mirror, Dumbledore told him that he saw a pair of socks, which Harry suspected as not being quite true. In their memorable reunion in King's Cross Station at the end of the seventh book, however, Dumbledore tells Harry his family's dark story, including how his sister, Ariana, died. And Harry finally realizes what Dumbledore would have seen in the Mirror of Erised: his family reunited and whole.[24] Of course, this was the same thing Harry saw—one of the many links between these two that bonded them so closely.

I believe this is why Albus Dumbledore chose the inscription he did for his mother and sister's tombstone: "*Where your treasure is, there will your heart be also.*"[25] The point is that Dumbledore's treasure—his deepest and most desperate desire—was to see his mother and sister again. And therefore, this is where his heart was and always would be. As he tells Harry, the death of his sister chastened him. It changed him. It snuffed out his desire for a magical ruling class (which was partly what led to his sister's death), and it caused him to devote his life to fighting those who were proponents of the vision for society he once championed—Grindelwald and Voldemort in particular. His heart was always set on this treasure—his family—and this gave him direction and shaped all the major decisions he made for the rest of his life.

This inscription found on the Dumbledores' tombstone also happens to be one of the two explicit references to the Bible in Harry Potter. It is a quote from Jesus, who uses it in a context of teaching on money (Matthew 6:21). Jesus' point is that a person can either store up physical treasures on earth, such as wealth and possessions, or they can store up treasures in heaven through serving God and joining his kingdom. But wherever the treasure is being stored up, that is where the person's heart will be. He goes on to say, "No one can serve two masters. Either you will hate the one and love the other, or you will be devoted to the one and despise the other. You cannot serve both God and money" (Matthew 6:24). Jesus is saying that we all have a treasure—something our heart desperately desires above all else—and we can be sure that our heart, or the orientation of our life, will be devoted to that treasure.

This is a major idea that can be found throughout the Bible. When the apostle Paul gives his diagnosis of what is wrong with the human race, he says that our fundamental problem is *idolatry*—that is, we worship things other than God (Romans 1:18–25). An idol is something you give your entire self to. It is that thing or person that is the deepest and most desperate desire of your heart. And because idols are created things, they are mortal and temporary (unlike the Creator, who is immortal). The Bible puts it this way:

> But their idols are silver and gold,
>   made by human hands.
> They have mouths, but cannot speak,
>   eyes, but cannot see.
> They have ears, but cannot hear,
>   noses, but cannot smell.
> They have hands, but cannot feel,
>   feet, but cannot walk,
>   nor can they utter a sound with their throats.
> Those who make them will be like them,
>   and so will all who trust in them. (Psalm 115:4–8)

Idols are dead, lifeless objects. They might look as though they are alive, but it is merely a façade. Now certainly there are not many people walking around in the United States today making gold and silver idols to worship, but we would be naïve to think that we are free from idolatry. If we looked into the Mirror of Erised, we would all find that we have a deep and desperate desire for something (though it might change from time to time!).

We worship things like money, power, sex, comfort, career success, family, health and fitness, beauty, affirmation from others, and political ideologies. And because all of these things are transient and none can last forever, they leave us feeling empty when we seek to find our meaning in them. This is what is meant by the line, "Those who make [idols] will be like them, / and so will all who trust in them." As idols are lifeless, so we become lifeless when we worship them. Or as another psalm puts it, "Those who run after other gods will suffer more and more" (Psalm 16:4).

The author David Foster Wallace, who was not himself a Christian, said it well:

> There is no such thing as not worshiping. Everybody worships. The only choice we get is what to worship. And the compelling reason for maybe choosing some sort of god or spiritual-type thing to worship . . . is that pretty much anything else you worship will eat you alive. If you worship money and things, if they are where you tap real meaning in life, then you will never have enough, never feel you have enough. It's the truth. Worship your body and beauty and sexual allure and you will always feel ugly. And when time and age start showing, you will die a million deaths before they finally grieve you. . . . Worship power, you will end up feeling weak and afraid, and you will need ever more power over others to numb you to your own fear. Worship your intellect, being seen as smart, you will end up feeling stupid, a fraud, always on the verge of being found out.[26]

Wallace's diagnosis is perceptive, yet bleak. Is there any alternative? After all, Dumbledore says, "The happiest man on earth would be able to use the Mirror of Erised like a normal mirror."[27] No deep, desperate desire—just his face. How would that be possible? What kind of person would be free from piercing desires for things in their life to change? How could a person have that level of contentment?

The Bible suggests an answer to this question. It teaches that standing behind the idols we worship are powers whom we are enslaved to.[28] And as long as these powers hold sway, we will continue to worship dehumanizing idols. We will continue to be consumed by our gazing at the Mirror of Erised—as Dumbledore says, "Men have wasted away before [the Mirror], entranced by what they have seen, or been driven mad."[29] We all know what this feels like: the gnawing ache of wanting what we do not have, or perhaps the paralyzing fear of losing what is precious to us. But the good news of the gospel is that Jesus defeated the powers behind our idols! As Jesus himself says, "Now is the time for judgment on this world; now the prince of this world will be driven out. And I, when I am lifted up from the earth, will draw all people to myself" (John 12:31–32).

The shocking part of this statement is that Jesus is talking about his crucifixion here (see John 12:33). That is what "lifted up" means—lifted up on a cross. Thus, Jesus is saying that he will defeat the prince of this world (and the other powers that stand behind the idols we worship) *by being crucified*. His crucifixion breaks their hold over the world because it deals with sin—the source of their power. And once the prince of this world is cast out, Jesus will draw all people to himself. The world will be free to worship him. In other words, the crucifixion of Jesus is the solution to the fundamental problem of the human race according to the Bible: worshiping God replaces worshiping idols. Because God is the Creator of the whole world, the only one in whom is life, worshiping him is life-*giving*, not life-draining. It is what we were made for.

So if we are imprisoned in a room gazing at the Mirror of Erised and consumed with anxiety, jealousy, and desperate longing for what we see, it is not because the door is locked. The prison guard has been bound and the door is wide open. To be freed from the captivating power of the idols we see in the Mirror, we need to see that they pale in comparison to the glory of God. And the Bible is clear that if we want to see the glory of God most fully displayed, we need to look at Jesus, and especially in the moment when he is crucified (John 12:27–28). This is the moment when we see what it means for God to be God in taking all the life-sucking consequences of human idolatry upon himself, even unto death. This is the moment when the author of life was killed to bring life to his world.

Only then—filled and energized by the life we find in Jesus—can we look into the Mirror of Erised and begin to use it as a normal mirror. Yes, the old images will come back and flicker before our eyes, accompanied by those old feelings of obsession and inadequacy. But because of what Jesus has done, we know that these idols have lost their power, and as we worship and pray, "Hallowed be your name," we will find that the images fade (Matthew 6:9).

4

Pure-Blooks

*We have a very different idea of what disgraces
the name of wizard, Malfoy.*

—Arthur Weasley[30]

It does not take long before Harry and Draco Malfoy become
sworn enemies during their first year at Hogwarts, but in their
second year the animosity heightens significantly. This is all fu-
eled by tensions surrounding "magical blood" and whether or
not it should play a role in determining a witch or wizard's status
in society. The sparks begin to fly when Malfoy calls Hermione
a Mudblood during an altercation on the Quidditch pitch and
Ron retaliates by casting a curse at Malfoy that backfires. Back in
Hagrid's hut, Ron, while intermittently vomiting slugs, explains,
"There are some wizards—like Malfoy's family—who think they're
better than everyone else because they're what people call pure-
blood."[31] This notion of pure-blood elitism plays a crucial role
throughout the second book, since Lucius Malfoy's plan to have
the Chamber of Secrets reopened is motivated by his desire to see
Hogwarts rid of Muggle-borns.

Such oppression towards Muggle-born witches and wizards
is a central tenet of Voldemort's vision for society. And when he ef-
fectively overthrows the Ministry of Magic in the seventh book, he

begins to enact this vision by setting up the Muggle-born Registration Commission, which brings Muggle-borns in for questioning, takes their wands, and sends them to Azkaban. It also prohibits Muggle-born children from attending Hogwarts. Voldemort's justification for such measures is that he sees Muggle-borns as pests that will slowly destroy the wizarding world if they are given the same status as pure-blood witches and wizards and permitted to learn magic.[32] The only solution is to dispose of them.

Muggles and nonhuman magical creatures are also victims of this oppression. The statue in the Atrium of the Ministry of Magic after Voldemort takes over displays this quite graphically, depicting a witch and wizard sitting on mounds of naked humans—a representation of where Muggles belong in this new world. House-elves are likewise treated poorly by Voldemort's regime, as Dobby explains to Harry: "Dobby remembers how it was when He-Who-Must-Not-Be-Named was at the height of his powers, sir! We house-elves were treated like vermin, sir!"[33] Goblins are forced to surrender control of Gringotts, and while giants and werewolves are used by Voldemort, they are treated as second-class creatures. The engraving on the statue at the Ministry of Magic sums up this pure-blood elitism well: "MAGIC IS MIGHT."[34]

This obsession with pure-blood status is obviously detrimental to those without magical blood, but it also makes those who do have this prejudice quite delusional. This is evident in the memory of Bob Ogden's trip to the Gaunts' shack near Little Hangleton. Ogden pulls out a summons for Morfin Gaunt to attend a disciplinary hearing, and Marvolo Gaunt, his father, absolutely loses his mind. Outraged that the Ministry thinks they can summon an ancient pure-blood family that is descended from Salazar Slytherin, he shows Ogden his ring engraved with the Peverell coat of arms and Salazar Slytherin's locket—the only two objects in his cottage that have any value—as if that settled the matter.[35] Marvolo Gaunt is an embittered, old man who lives in a pathetic shack, but he still believes he deserves special treatment from the Ministry because of his generations-long pure-blood ancestry.

In the face of this pure-blood elitism, however, the heroes in Harry Potter argue that the "purity" of one's blood does not matter. This is why they resist Voldemort's rise to power in the Second Wizarding War. And no one champions this ideology more than Albus Dumbledore. Dumbledore shares his views very clearly in response to Cornelius Fudge's prejudiced statement against giants: "You place too much importance, and you always have done, on the so-called purity of blood! You fail to recognize that it matters not what someone is born, but what they grow to be!"[36]

Furthermore, Dumbledore does not merely hold this view in the abstract; he puts it into practice by hiring werewolves (Lupin), half-giants (Hagrid), and centaurs (Firenze) to teach at Hogwarts; paying house-elves (Dobby) to work at Hogwarts; and developing meaningful relationships with merpeople. Others share Dumbledore's practice of treating Muggle-borns, Muggles, and nonhuman magical creatures with dignity, and it earns them the title of "blood traitors" (so named because these witches and wizards have betrayed the purity of their blood by associating with those who are not pure-blood or at least half-blood).

As in Harry Potter, a major theme in the biblical story is bloodline. It all begins with the Israelites, who are set apart by God as his chosen people through whom he would bless the entire world and rescue it from the curse it is under because of human sin. This is made clear by God in a promise that he makes to Abraham, the father of the nation of Israel:

> I will make you into a great nation,
>   and I will bless you;
> I will make your name great,
>   and you will be a blessing.
> I will bless those who bless you,
>   and whoever curses you I will curse;
> and all peoples on earth
>   will be blessed through you. (Genesis 12:2–3)

The Israelites were to function as a "kingdom of priests" to the world by bearing witness to who God is and what he is like (Exodus 19:4–6). But unfortunately, this privileged role in God's plan to bless all nations becomes a source of pride for the people of Israel, and they begin to see themselves as superior to the nations around them.

This is illustrated very clearly in the story of Jonah. Jonah is a prophet of Israel who is told to go to the pagan city of Nineveh to tell them about God's judgment that is coming upon them because of their violent ways. But because he does not like the Ninevites, he disobeys God and does not go. Eventually, though, after God gets his attention through a storm and sending a fish to save him from drowning, Jonah goes to Nineveh and gives its residents the message from God. And shockingly, the Ninevites repent, and God relents from the judgment he had intended. But Jonah becomes angry at this—so angry he wishes he were dead. He wanted to see God judge these cruel pagans, and his privileged identity is threatened by the fact that God has shown favor to non-Israelites. It is a sad sight to behold. Jonah's world is crumbling, and he sounds quite as delusional as Marvolo Gaunt by presuming that he should be treated specially by God because of his "pure-blood" Israelite status.

By the time of Jesus, these same prejudices were rampant. Many Jews believed that their bloodline gave them a special status over the wicked and impure Gentiles who lived around them. In response to this, John the Baptist, the prophet sent to prepare Israel for the coming of Jesus, warned them that their ancestry would not cause God to judge them more leniently: "And do not think you can say to yourselves, 'We have Abraham as our father.' I tell you that out of these stones God can raise up children for Abraham" (Matthew 3:9).

And in this same vein, Jesus' mission was one that extended to both Jews and Gentiles. He healed and taught and ate with both Jews and Gentiles during his ministry on earth, and his death and resurrection reconciled both Jews and Gentiles to God. It is on this basis that Jews and Gentiles are reconciled to each other as well. The apostle Paul explains,

> For [Jesus] himself is our peace, who has made the two
> groups one and has destroyed the barrier, the dividing

> wall of hostility, by setting aside in his flesh the law with
> its commands and regulations. His purpose was to create
> in himself one new humanity out of the two, thus making
> peace, and in one body to reconcile both of them to God
> through the cross, by which he put to death their hostil-
> ity. (Ephesians 2:14–16)

Because both Jews and Gentiles are reconciled to God in the same way—through Jesus Christ—they are consequently brought together and reconciled to one another. Paul will go on to say that both Jews and Gentiles are members of God's "household" or family (Ephesians 2:19), but this family is born "not of blood nor of the will of the flesh nor of the will of man, but of God" (John 1:13 ESV). This family is defined not by its natural bloodline but by the blood of Jesus and by God's Spirit who lives inside them, marking them as God's children.

As it so happened, this issue of bloodlines was arguably the most difficult issue that the church struggled with in its infancy. Despite the example of Jesus, Jewish Christians were hesitant to break their ritual purity laws and eat with Gentiles, and therefore it took three visions for the apostle Peter to be willing to step foot inside a Gentile household to share the gospel with them (Acts 10). Furthermore, the first major controversy that the church had to deal with was how Jewish Christians and Gentile Christians would interact with each other as a part of the same family (Acts 15). One only has to look at how often Paul's letters deal with the subject of unity between Jews and Gentiles to realize this was a major issue.

The issue of unequal treatment on the basis of bloodlines is still one that plagues the church all across the world today, including in the United States. This is part of the dark history of the American church, as Jemar Tisby points out: "Racism has colored the character of the American church for the past four hundred years."[37] And it continues into the present day as white Christians ignore their non-white brothers and sisters who have been bruised and battered by various forms of systemic racism in this country, much like the priest and the Levite in Jesus' parable of the good Samaritan who walk right by the man left for dead (Luke 10:25–37).

It must be noted that this is not merely a failure to follow a command given to us as Christians—such as loving our neighbors as ourselves (though it is that as well!). At a deeper level, it is a failure to live out our identity as a family where "there is no Gentile or Jew, circumcised or uncircumcised, barbarian, Scythian, slave or free, but Christ is all, and is in all" (Colossians 3:11).[38]

The Christian response to racism is that we of all people should follow Jesus' example as "blood traitors"—in this case confronting white supremacy instead of "pure-blood supremacy." We should be those who pursue the unity of the church across racial, ethnic, and national lines and who confront those, as the apostle Paul did, who put that unity in jeopardy either by their prejudice or indifference—because if we do not, we are saying with our actions that "Christ died for nothing" (Galatians 2:21).

And as we do this, we must never lose sight of the hope we have that one day the church in all its diversity will live together in perfect love and unity. Though Dumbledore did not live to witness it, after Voldemort was vanquished for good, Dumbledore's vision was finally fulfilled for one glorious morning: When the Great Hall was restored and the survivors were feasting in celebration, they were not split according to house or even according to whether they were human or not. "All were jumbled together."[39] The house-elves had come up from the kitchens. The centaurs had come out of the forest. Even Grawp joined in the festivities.

The final vision of the church is similar: we see "a great multitude that no one could count, from every nation, tribe, people and language, standing before the throne and before the Lamb" (Revelation 7:9). In other words, the church is the true fulfillment of Dumbledore's vision that "it matters not what someone is born, but what they grow to be"—namely, followers of Jesus and children of the living God.[40]

5

Horcruxes

You must understand that the soul is supposed to remain intact and whole.

—HORACE SLUGHORN[41]

NOT UNTIL THE END of the sixth book do we discover what it will take to finally defeat Lord Voldemort: his Horcruxes must be destroyed. This is revealed through the memory of a conversation that takes place between Horace Slughorn and Tom Riddle. Slughorn is taken aback that Tom wants to discuss such dark magic, but eventually he acquiesces and tells Tom that a Horcrux is an object that has been transformed to encase a portion of a person's soul. Tom wonders how it is possible for the soul to be split in such a way, to which Slughorn answers, "Splitting it is an act of violation, it is against nature. . . . [The soul is split] by an act of evil—the supreme act of evil. By committing murder."[42]

This is why Horcruxes are one of the darkest forms of magic—creating one requires that you murder another human being. Intriguingly though, Slughorn explains that murder splits the soul because it is a violation of *nature*. "Nature" in the Harry Potter world apparently has some kind of moral code embedded in it such that when someone transgresses that code, they inflict damage on themselves.

The Bible is actually very similar in how it speaks about evil. People sometimes talk about God's moral laws as if they were put in place simply to keep people from having fun and enjoying themselves. Understood this way, God's moral laws are arbitrary joy-kills. In reality, however, God's moral laws reflect the "grain of the universe." That is, because God is the Creator and designed the universe to work a certain way, if you break his laws, you are going against the grain and will inflict damage upon yourself (and oftentimes others). There is a world of difference between these two ways of understanding sin—the same distinction as that between a police officer pulling you over for speeding around a really tight turn and flying off a cliff because you were speeding around a really tight turn.

Humanity discovered this the hard way in the garden of Eden. Adam, the first human, was commanded by God, "You are free to eat from any tree in the garden; but you must not eat from the tree of the knowledge of good and evil, for when you eat from it you will certainly die" (Genesis 2:16–17). Adam is given quite a bit of latitude—only one tree in the entire garden is off-limits to him.

In the very next chapter, however, a serpent approaches Eve, Adam's wife, and tempts her to eat fruit from this tree. Adam and Eve both give in and eat fruit from the tree, and the passage says, "Then the eyes of both of them were opened, and they realized they were naked; so they sewed fig leaves together and made coverings for themselves" (Genesis 3:7). God was right—Adam and Eve's disobedience led to death. Not only were they exiled from the garden of Eden and cut off from the tree of life (the antidote to death), even in that moment the intimate relationship that Adam and Eve had with each other died as they sought to hide themselves from each other. And the same thing happened to the intimate relationship they had with God: "Then the man and his wife heard the sound of the LORD God as he was walking in the garden in the cool of the day, and they hid from the LORD God among the trees of the garden" (Genesis 3:8). There was a fracture that took place in Adam and Eve because they disobeyed God. They had gone against the grain of the universe.

The Bible teaches that all humans are in this condition. The apostle Paul writes, "As for you, you were dead in your transgressions and sins" (Ephesians 2:1). Of course, we are all physically alive, but Paul is saying that we are, in a sense, dead because of the sin and evil we have done. We have damaged and fractured our humanity. Sin dehumanizes us, just as Dumbledore observed in Voldemort: "Voldemort has seemed to grow less human with the passing years," which Dumbledore concludes is only possible if he has decimated his soul through very dark magic.[43] It is therefore not just others who are harmed by the evil we do—our souls pay a price.

In Harry Potter, the soul is split through the "supreme act of evil," which is murder. But lest one think that it is only the evil of murder that damages one's self, Jesus himself says,

> You have heard that it was said to the people long ago, "You shall not murder, and anyone who murders will be subject to judgment." But I tell you that anyone who is angry with a brother or sister will be subject to judgment. Again, anyone who says to a brother or sister, "Raca,"[44] is answerable to the court. And anyone who says, "You fool!" will be in danger of the fire of hell. (Matthew 5:21–22)

Jesus is saying that if you merely get angry with another human being or treat them with contempt, it is an evil that will bring destruction upon yourself.

Once the soul has been torn apart, is there any way for it to be put back together? This is the question that Ron asks Hermione just before they set off with Harry to hunt Horcruxes. Hermione, who has been doing her research, says that there is, but that it would be utter agony. Given all the magical ways one can induce pain, Harry and Ron probably think that Hermione is about to tell them about some spell that a person must perform on themselves or a potion they must drink. But when Harry asks what you have to do, Hermione responds, "Remorse . . . You've got to really feel what you've done."[45] She adds that a footnote indicates the pain can be so severe that it will kill you.

The soul is put back together by *remorse*. And you can only have remorse when you have felt the weight of what you have done—a painful experience indeed. But Hermione's research also suggests that remorse is very powerful—on par with Basilisk venom, which is one of the only ways that a Horcrux can be destroyed. It is pain that leads to tremendous change.

We see this play out during a crucial moment in Harry's life—just after Dobby has been killed. Before the house-elf died, Harry had been fixated on the idea of finding the Deathly Hallows and using them to defeat Voldemort, despite the fact that Dumbledore had given him a mission to destroy Voldemort's Horcruxes. But after Dobby dies, his perspective changes. While he is digging Dobby's grave and contemplating his plan of action, he realizes that his all-consuming desire for the Hallows has dissipated; grief has taken its place. And Harry sees the foolishness of his former Hallows obsession. Dobby's death was like a shot of cold water that brought him to his senses.[46] It is only then that Harry begins to think clearly again and changes course to hunting Horcruxes.

The Bible likewise teaches that the pain of remorse must be felt in order for a person to change or repent (the word "repent" in the Bible means to change direction, to stop going one way and to go another). The apostle Paul puts it like this in a letter to a group of Christians:

> Even if I caused you sorrow by my letter, I do not regret it. Though I did regret it—I see that my letter hurt you, but only for a little while—yet now I am happy, not because you were made sorry, but because your sorrow led you to repentance. For you became sorrowful as God intended and so were not harmed in any way by us. Godly sorrow brings repentance that leads to salvation and leaves no regret, but worldly sorrow brings death. See what this godly sorrow has produced in you: what earnestness, what eagerness to clear yourselves, what indignation, what alarm, what longing, what concern, what readiness to see justice done. At every point you have proved yourselves to be innocent in this matter. (2 Corinthians 7:8–11)

Paul had previously written a letter to this church in which he had rebuked them for their immoral behavior. In one sense, he did not want to rebuke them because he knew it would cause them pain. But he knew that pain—"godly sorrow" as he calls it—had to be experienced in order for them to repent and change.

Paul differentiates between "godly" sorrow and "worldly" sorrow, and I think the difference between the two is this: worldly sorrow is when a person is simply sorry that they have been caught or sorry for the consequences that their actions have caused them, while godly sorrow is when they are truly remorseful and feel the weight of what they have done. Paul says that after this church was rebuked, they really did feel remorse or godly sorrow for what they had done. And the sign of it was that they repented and changed their behavior.

Both Harry Potter and the Bible teach that you must experience the pain of remorse in order to change. And Hermione even adds that the pain of it can kill you. But the Bible teaches that the pain of it *will* kill you because you must go through a death to change. We do not just need a little tinkering to get back on track. Our situation is far more dire.

Jesus said, "Whoever wants to be my disciple must deny themselves and take up their cross and follow me. For whoever wants to save their life will lose it, but whoever loses their life for me and the gospel will save it" (Mark 8:34–35). The point is clear. The way to life—to being put back together and healed—is through death. Not a physical death, but a death to that part of us that is dark and evil.[47] The words of the prophecy are fitting here: "Neither can live while the other survives."[48] Either the darkness in us must die or, like a Horcrux, it will slowly destroy us. It is as if healing and wholeness are on the other side of a fast-flowing river that we can neither swim nor bridge by our own moral efforts. The only way across? "Jesus plunged into the river and, being well and truly drowned, was carried to the farther shore. And he told his disciples to follow him."[49]

This remorse that leads to repentance is how the Christian life begins. When Jesus went around preaching the gospel, he said,

"The time has come . . . . The kingdom of God has come near. Repent and believe the good news!" (Mark 1:15). In other words, "You're going the wrong way! Turn around, and come be a part of the project I am launching to rescue the world. And find that in it you will be rescued yourself." But this is not just how the Christian life starts—it is how it is lived. This is why Jesus taught his followers to daily pray, "Forgive us our debts, as we also have forgiven our debtors" (Matthew 6:12). We regularly need to ask for forgiveness and repent of the wrongs we do, and this entails remorse: feeling the weight of what it is that we have done.

Perhaps the pain of remorse is a barrier to you repenting and believing the gospel. Maybe you do not want to take an honest look at the things you have done that have fractured both yourself and others because you do not want to give them up and it is more comfortable to justify your actions. Or perhaps you are a Christian, but there is a part of your life that you do not want to bring into the light because of how painful remorse might be. The gospel does not alleviate our fears at this point; it does not promise that repentance will be painless. But it does promise that there is healing on the other side, just as a doctor might have to cause temporary pain in order to facilitate healing. As Jesus said, "It is not the healthy who need a doctor, but the sick. I have not come to call the righteous, but sinners to repentance" (Luke 5:32).

6

The Deathly Hallows

The ancient story refers to three objects, or Hallows, which, if united, will make the possessor master of Death.

—XENOPHILIUS LOVEGOOD[50]

PEOPLE WHO STUDY LEADERSHIP have noted that there are many different kinds of power. Some examples include the power of position, the power of knowledge or expertise, and the power of influence. Of course, there is also simply the power of physical strength. In the wizarding world, there is another dimension to power that must be considered: magical power. This can be broken down further according to the different branches of magic that one can master, such as Transfiguration, Charms, Potions, and Defense Against the Dark Arts. But in Harry Potter, even in a world with incredibly powerful witches and wizards, power is redefined in a surprising way.

Throughout the series, there is unanimous agreement that Dumbledore is the most powerful wizard in the world. Even Voldemort acknowledges his greatness, as Minerva McGonagall tells Dumbledore in the very first chapter: "Everyone knows you're the only one You-Know- oh, all right, *Voldemort*, was frightened of."[51] And we witness quite awesome displays of Dumbledore's power as the series goes on.

One example that stands out is at the end of the fourth book when Barty Crouch Jr. (appearing as Mad-Eye Moody) is about to kill Harry in Moody's office. Just before he casts his spell, however, Dumbledore fires a stunning spell that blasts through the door and hits Barty Crouch Jr. on the spot:

> At that moment, Harry fully understood for the first time why people said Dumbledore was the only wizard Volde-mort had ever feared. The look upon Dumbledore's face as he stared down at the unconscious form of Mad-Eye Moody was more terrible than Harry could have ever imagined. . . . A sense of power radiated from Dumb-ledore as though he were giving off burning heat.[52]

Dumbledore is often warm and gentle, but this should not be mistaken for weakness. When his students are threatened, Dumbledore means business.

Another moment that stands out is at the end of the fifth book when Dumbledore shows up at the Ministry of Magic to rescue Harry, his friends, and some members of the Order of the Phoenix from the Death Eaters. It does not matter that the Death Eaters have a two-to-one advantage in numbers; when they see Dumbledore, they all scramble in fear and do not even try to put up a fight while Dumbledore ties them up easily with his wand. And then he showcases the full gamut of his magical ability in his epic duel with Voldemort in the Atrium of the Ministry of Magic by enchanting the different fountain statues to protect Harry, send for the Aurors, pin Bellatrix to the ground, and fight Voldemort—an awe-inspiring display of power.

But it is not just the magnitude of Dumbledore's power that stands out in each of these scenes; another common element in them is that Dumbledore uses his prodigious power to help and save others. He uses his authority as Hogwarts Headmaster and leader of the Order of the Phoenix similarly. While he certainly gives daunting assignments to teachers and members of the Order (such as sending Hagrid and Madame Maxime to the giants, Lupin to the werewolves, and Snape to the Death Eaters), it is evident that he cares about and values each of them, and the tasks he gives are always for the purpose of protecting others from Voldemort's malice. And clearly Dumbledore is lifted up as an admirable example of how one *should* use their power.

Other characters in Harry Potter do not use their power so admirably. Voldemort, of course, is one example. But even other seemingly "good" characters do not use their power well. Cornelius Fudge and Rufus Scrimgeour, for instance, use their power and influence to snuff out the truth and give the public a falsely positive perception of how the wizarding world is faring against Voldemort. And Sirius Black notes that Barty Crouch's cruel treatment of his house-elf, Winky, is a good indicator of what he is really like (though there is a bit of irony in this statement, since Sirius does not treat *his* house-elf, Kreacher, very well).[53] The point here is that bad leaders deceive and dominate those under their authority, while good leaders use their power to serve others— particularly those who are vulnerable.

But Dumbledore did not always use his power this way. Nor is he naïve about the way power could still corrupt him. He recounts all this to Harry when they meet in King's Cross Station at the end of the seventh book. Because he showed such lust for power as a young man when conspiring with Gellert Grindelwald to create a magical ruling class, he tells Harry that he turned down the post of Minister of Magic multiple times. It presented temptations that he did not think he could resist. He goes on to say that perhaps the people "best suited to power are those who have never sought it"—people who embrace leadership because they are compelled to and find that they handle it well.[54] People like Harry. It seems counterintuitive and certainly countercultural, but, according to Dumbledore, a certain humility is required to bear the heavy burden of leadership.

Jesus' teaching on power is very similar. On the night before his crucifixion, he ate a final meal with his disciples, during which he broke bread and shared wine to symbolize that his body was about to be broken and his blood shed. It was a deeply personal and intimate moment. But immediately after this, his disciples got into an argument:

> A dispute also arose among them as to which of them
> was considered to be greatest. Jesus said to them, "The
> kings of the Gentiles lord it over them; and those who
> exercise authority over them call themselves Benefac-
> tors. But you are not to be like that. Instead, the greatest
> among you should be like the youngest, and the one who
> rules like the one who serves. For who is greater, the one
> who is at the table or the one who serves? Is it not the
> one who is at the table? But I am among you as one who
> serves." (Luke 22:24–27)

The disciples did not get it. Jesus had just illustrated the significance of what he was about to do in dying for them, and they were
arguing over who was the greatest. So Jesus flips their categories.
He says that whoever wants to have power in the kingdom of God
must serve and give of themselves to others. Those who wish to
be great must become lowly. And Jesus did not just teach this—he
embodied it. Though he was God and had supreme power over all,
he gave his life to save others. He demonstrated that those in power
should be known for the way they serve others, not the way others serve them. He inverted the pattern that was widely practiced
among the kings of his day and which is just as widespread today.

The message of Harry Potter is not just that self-sacrifice
qualifies one to be in power, however; it goes a step further and
says that there is great power *in* self-sacrifice. This is all part of the
magic of the Deathly Hallows. The Deathly Hallows are the three
objects—the Elder Wand, the Resurrection Stone, and the Invisibility Cloak—which, when united, make one the master of death.
But surprisingly, simply possessing the Hallows does not unleash
their true power. This is why Dumbledore tells Harry, "Maybe a
man in a million could unite the Hallows."[55] Though Dumbledore
took the Elder Wand from Grindelwald to protect others from
his violence and destruction, he took the Invisibility Cloak and
the Resurrection Stone for selfish reasons, and thus he says these
Hallows would not have had the same power for him as they did
for Harry, who used them to enable his final sacrifice. The possessor's motivation for taking and using the Hallows makes all the
difference.

It is natural to think of the Elder Wand as the chief of the three Hallows. This, after all, is how Jesus says the world does power: "The kings of the Gentiles lord it over them." The way that people often gain and hold their power is through domination and force, goals that are more easily attained with an unbeatable wand. But "The Tale of the Three Brothers" suggests that the Deathly Hallows do not work this way. The Hallow that protects its owner from Death is not the Elder Wand but the Invisibility Cloak, the "true magic" of which, unlike either of the other Hallows, is that it can hide and protect others, as Dumbledore points out.[56] Embedded within the legendary origin story of the Deathly Hallows, then, is the notion that shielding and serving others (what the Invisibility Cloak can do) is more powerful than dominating others (what the Elder Wand can do). This is why the magic of the Deathly Hallows is unleashed through self-sacrifice, the uttermost form of shielding and serving others. And this is why Dumbledore tells Harry, "You are the worthy possessor of the Hallows"—because he used them to enable his self-sacrifice and not for personal gain.[57]

Voldemort did not understand this. After failing to defeat Harry in two successive encounters—first with his own wand in the Little Hangleton graveyard and then again with a borrowed wand in the escape from Privet Drive to the safe house—Voldemort believed the problem was Harry's wand. And so he went on a quest for the wand that was said to be invincible. What he failed to realize is that the power Harry possessed—the power that made his wand so strong that it beat Voldemort's when they connected in the graveyard—was that of his love, his courageous self-sacrifice.[58] Power that could unite the Deathly Hallows and make one master of death.

The Bible uses a very striking image to illustrate the power in self-sacrifice. There is a climactic vision in the book of Revelation where God is sitting on his throne and holding a sealed scroll in his hand (a symbol of God's plan to rescue the world), and an angel proclaims, "Who is worthy to break the seals and open the scroll?" (Revelation 5:2). No one in the whole universe is found to be worthy, which causes John, the one receiving this vision, to begin to weep.

But then someone says to him, "Do not weep! See, the Lion of the tribe of Judah, the Root of David, has triumphed. He is able to open the scroll and its seven seals" (Revelation 5:5). But when John looks up, he does not see a lion. He writes, "Then I saw a Lamb, looking as if it had been slain, standing at the center of the throne" (Revelation 5:6). In place of a lion, a symbol of great power, John sees a lamb, a symbol of humility and self-sacrifice. The lamb represents Jesus, and the purpose of the vision is to illustrate that there is great, lion-like power in Jesus' crucifixion. The slaying of the lamb may have looked like a moment of weakness, but as the apostle Paul says, "The weakness of God is stronger than human strength" (1 Corinthians 1:25).

In a magical world of great spells and extraordinary displays of power, the message of Harry Potter is that self-sacrifice is what fits one to be in power and lead well. But it also says that true power can be found within self-sacrifice, power formidable enough to unite the Deathly Hallows. In Jesus, we get a stunning picture of what this looks like as he manifests his power, not as a lion, but as a lamb who was slain.

But Jesus does not just embody this kind of power; he also calls those who follow him to learn and practice it. This, of course, is immensely important and relevant for how we think about leadership. What if more leaders took Dumbledore's words to heart—that perhaps those "best suited to power are those who have never sought it"?[59] In a day when it is normal to hear about leaders exploiting their power with regards to sex, money, or verbal abuse, this approach to power would fundamentally alter the world. It would transform leadership as we know it. And it would surely make following these leaders—whether in the church or elsewhere in the world—a far more attractive prospect. The duties of followership might still be demanding, but as in the case of Dumbledore, having a self-sacrificial leader makes all the difference.

The power that Christians possess is not in swords and weapons, in asserting themselves over others, in winning debates or elections, or even in their numbers. It is in self-sacrifice. This is the power that conquers the evil at work in the world: "They triumphed over [the evil one] by the blood of the Lamb and by the word of their testimony; they did not love their lives so much as to shrink from death" (Revelation 12:11).

PART II

The Characters

7

Harry, Ron, and Hermione

Finally, he saw the two whose company he craved most.[60]

A BRIEF SURVEY OF the most popular books and movies today will reveal that the most significant relationships in these stories are almost always romantic. You will of course see this in Disney movies and romantic comedies, but even in action movies, such as those in the Marvel Cinematic Universe, romantic relationships are central. Love stories undoubtedly have a certain spellbinding quality that captures our hearts, which is why they figure so prominently. But what are often noticeably absent are deep friendships devoid of romance.

Harry Potter is different. In this story, a balance is struck in that there are many romances and marriages, but there are also plenty of rich, meaningful friendships. Moreover, a number of key characters—Dumbledore, Snape, Sirius, and Hagrid, to name a few—never marry for different reasons (though some of them do have romantic interests). And most significantly, the paramount relationships in the story are the friendships that form between Harry, Ron, and Hermione. Though Ron and Hermione do eventually become interested in each other and get married, it is the *friendship* between these three that is at the heart of the story, not the eventual romance.

This is why reading Harry Potter is like a breath of fresh air. In a culture saturated with romantic love, but which knows very little of intimate friendship, Harry Potter gives us a beautiful vision of what friendship can look like. In his classic book on the different kinds of love, C. S. Lewis puts it well: "Those who cannot conceive Friendship as a substantive love but only as a disguise or elaboration of Eros [sexual love] betray the fact that they have never had a friend."[61] Perhaps it is because our culture is starved for true friendship that the only type of love we can relate to is romantic love. With this backdrop, the friendship between Harry, Ron, and Hermione as they journey together through a myriad of perilous challenges to defeat evil is awe-inspiring.

The story of how these three become friends is quite memorable. They start off on rocky footing because Harry and Ron are annoyed by Hermione's bossy, "know-it-all" attitude. On one such occasion, Hermione is brought to tears when she overhears Ron making fun of her and takes refuge in the girls' bathroom. But when Harry and Ron hear that a mountain troll has been set loose in the school, they make for the bathroom to try to rescue Hermione, and, with a bit of luck, they manage to take the troll down. "From that moment on, Hermione Granger became their friend. There are some things you can't share without ending up liking each other, and knocking out a twelve-foot mountain troll is one of them."[62]

Their friendship certainly has its ups and downs. They go through various fights and quarrels that keep some combination of two of them from speaking to each other, but they also rise to great heights and go on adventures together to keep Lord Voldemort and his followers at bay. Mostly though, they simply enjoy each other's company and help each other through the daily grind at Hogwarts.

A change takes place, however, in the sixth book, when the stakes of their friendship are raised. Just before school starts, Dumbledore takes Harry aside and tells him that he wants to give him private lessons that will help Harry defeat Voldemort. He follows that up by telling Harry that he should tell Ron and Hermione about the prophecy and confide in them what he learns during his lessons. Harry begins to object, citing the fact that he does not want to worry or frighten them. But Dumbledore insightfully recognizes that maybe what Harry does not want to admit to his friends is that *he* is worried and frightened. Dumbledore rightly points out that these are precisely the times when we need our friends most.[63]

Here Dumbledore identifies one of the essential characteristics of friendship: *transparency*.[64] Of course, there is risk here. Making yourself known to your friends, particularly in your weaknesses, opens up the possibility that they will think less of you and perhaps even pull away from the friendship. But if you do not make yourself known, it is impossible to have friends.

This is why Voldemort can never have a true friend. Even from a young age, the boy Voldemort was highly self-sufficient and refused the help of anyone, such as when he declined Dumbledore's offer to help him buy his school things in Diagon Alley (even though he knew nothing about the wizarding world). The same is true of the adult Voldemort. He certainly has followers whom he identifies as his "friends," but Dumbledore shrewdly points out that he treats them more like servants. They do not really know what he is up to—even if they claim to be in his inner circle. As Dumbledore says, none of them would be able to give an account of what Voldemort did in the mysterious years after he left Hogwarts.[65]

No one knows much about his life because he does not want to share it with anyone. He is so obsessed with preserving himself and his power that he cannot fathom being dependent on anyone or anything. This is why Dumbledore says, "Voldemort has never had a friend, nor do I believe that he has ever wanted one."[66] To Voldemort, having a friend would be a sign of weakness.

But because Harry does make himself known to his friends, he is able to receive the blessing of the other essential characteristic of friendship: *constancy*. When Harry tells Ron and Hermione about the prophecy, they do not pull away. They sit with him and comfort him, and their response has a visceral effect on Harry: A sense of peace begins to radiate through his body. The weight on his shoulders begins to lift because he feels like he is no longer carrying it alone.[67] The loyalty of friends can steel our hearts to face danger like nothing else.

Even still, when Harry decides he is going to hunt Horcruxes instead of coming back to Hogwarts for his seventh year, he wants to take the quest alone. But Ron and Hermione flat out refuse to let him do this. As Ron puts it, "We're with you whatever happens."[68] And they back up their promise with action. Both take significant measures to protect their families: Hermione modifies her parents' memories so that they will move to Australia, and she is unsure if she will ever see them again, while Ron transforms the ghoul in his attic to look like him so that people will not accuse his family of helping Harry. Once again, Harry is deeply moved by the loyalty of his friends and the sacrifices they make to come with him.[69] You take a great risk when making yourself known to friends and relying on them, but when they love you in return, the effect can be quite poignant, as Harry experienced.

Though many people know intuitively that these two characteristics—transparency and constancy—are essential components of friendship, the Bible highlights their importance as well. The book of Proverbs tells us, "Perfume and incense bring joy to the heart, and the pleasantness of a friend springs from their heartfelt advice" (27:9). The point—just as perfume is sweet-smelling, so a friend's advice is pleasant because they know our hearts. It fits our need because there is transparency in the friendship.

Proverbs also tells us, "A friend loves at all times, and a brother is born for a time of adversity" (17:17). The point here is that relatives may be there for us when we are in need, but a friend is always there for us. They are constantly at our side. And the effect this type of friendship can have on a person is found in another proverb: "One who has unreliable friends soon comes to ruin, but there is a friend who sticks closer than a brother" (18:24). If you do not want your life to fall off the rails, it is essential to have friendships that are marked by both transparency and constancy. Pastor Tim Keller says it well:

> To be loved but not known is comforting but superficial.
> To be known and not loved is our greatest fear. But to
> be fully known and truly loved is, well, a lot like being
> loved by God. It is what we need more than anything.
> It liberates us from pretense, humbles us out of our self-
> righteousness, and fortifies us for any difficulty life can
> throw at us.[70]

Harry, Ron, and Hermione certainly experienced the power of friendship fortifying them against the difficulties of life, but the reason they encountered these difficulties in the first place is because they dared to stand up to Lord Voldemort and his followers. And of course, when you stand up to evil, evil fights back. This is why Ron's and Hermione's friendship was so meaningful and precious to Harry—it meant that he did not have to face this evil alone.

Thus, the transparency and constancy that Harry, Ron, and Hermione shared was about more than just getting to know each other and sharing life together—though they certainly did that as well. The deep friendship they forged ultimately became what it was because they had a mission they were pursuing together, and the most heroic displays of the power of their friendship came in the context of the adventures they went on and the challenges they faced as a part of that mission.

It is the same with the biblical vision of friendship. Biblical friendship is not just about sharing life together, as important as that is. It is much bigger, and indeed more exhilarating, than that. Biblical friendship is about having a shared mission—the apostle Paul calls it "partnership in the gospel" (Philippians 1:5). When a person becomes a Christian, they join the Spirit-filled community through whom God is building his kingdom on earth as it is in heaven. And as God's kingdom is being built, it should come as no surprise that rival kingdoms fight back. *This* is the context of the biblical vision of friendship. These friendships are characterized by transparency and constancy, but the transparency and constancy are made all the more meaningful and precious because these friends are supporting one another through the hardships and adventures of proclaiming and embodying the kingdom of God.

The Bible does not just say that we partner with *each other* in this mission, though; it says that we have entered into partnership or "fellowship" with Jesus (1 Corinthians 1:9). And in partnering with Jesus, we find him to be the greatest of friends. When Jesus was about to die, he said to his followers, "I no longer call you servants, because a servant does not know his master's business. Instead, I have called you *friends*, for everything that I learned from my Father I have made known to you" (John 15:15). Jesus embodies transparency and invites his followers to play a meaningful role in his mission. And he shows the constancy of his friendship when he says, "Greater love has no one than this: to lay down one's life for one's friends" (John 15:13). Jesus loved his friends all the way unto death. But the Bible also teaches that he rose again, ascended into heaven, and "is at the right hand of God . . . interceding for us" (Romans 8:34). That is, he is praying for us even now. He is the friend who never fails.

And so, when we see the inspiring, devoted friendship between Harry, Ron, and Hermione, we should not only seek this kind of friendship in our own lives, we should see an echo of the friendship of Jesus—the one who, because he rose again, makes friendship immortal. "This is the comfort of friends, that though they may be said to die, yet their friendship and society are, in the best sense, ever present, because immortal."[71]

8

Lily

Not only was she a singularly gifted witch, she was also an uncommonly kind woman. She had a way of seeing the beauty in others even, and perhaps most especially, when that person could not see it in themselves.

—REMUS LUPIN[72]

WITHOUT QUESTION, ONE OF the main themes in the Harry Potter series is love—particularly self-sacrificial love. And one of the characters who is frequently praised for her display of sacrificial love is Lily Potter. We never actually meet Lily in the flesh because she dies at the beginning of the story, but we learn about her through the memories of those who knew her well. And one thing is clear: she was a very gifted witch. But she may have been even more gifted than many people thought because she understood the mysterious workings of the magical world so well.

We first learn of Lily's sacrifice at the end of the first book when Dumbledore explains to Harry why Quirrell was unable to touch him: "Your mother died to save you. . . . To have been loved so deeply, even though the person who loved us is gone, will give us some protection forever."[73] Her love functioned as a repellent against the hatred that filled Quirrell (possessed by Voldemort at the time).

This is also why Voldemort's Killing Curse failed in the first place and rebounded when he tried to kill baby Harry: Lily's sacrifice for her son gave him magical, lasting protection. And interestingly, the power of this love lies in Lily's shed *blood*. This is why Dumbledore asked Lily's sister, Petunia, to take Harry in and raise him. He explains to Harry,

> Your mother's sacrifice made the bond of blood the strongest shield I could give you. . . . While you can still call home the place where your mother's blood dwells, there you cannot be touched or harmed by Voldemort. He shed her blood, but it lives on in you and her sister. Her blood became your refuge.[74]

To overcome this protection, Voldemort uses Harry's own blood to form his new body in the Little Hangleton graveyard. And it works—Voldemort is able to touch Harry. But little does he know that it will be his undoing. Because the power of Lily's protection is in her blood, when Voldemort took Harry's blood, he also filled himself with the power of Lily's sacrifice. As Dumbledore explains to Harry at the end of the seventh book, "He tethered you to life while he lives!"[75] Taking Harry's blood did not ultimately overcome Lily's protection, then; it only strengthened it, thus making it impossible for Voldemort to kill Harry.

Behind all this talk of sacrifice and blood, though, is the idea that love is the most powerful form of magic in the wizarding world. This is at the very heart of the divide between Dumbledore and Voldemort. In one conversation, Voldemort boasts of the extraordinary and unprecedented magic he has experimented in, to which Dumbledore replies that Voldemort remains woefully ignorant of other forms of magic. Voldemort sneers, "Nothing I have seen in the world has supported your famous pronouncements that love is more powerful than my kind of magic."[76]

But of course, Dumbledore is right. The sacrifice Lily made winds up being Voldemort's downfall. It is a magic that is even more powerful than death, since its power lingers long after Lily has died and protects Harry from Voldemort's Killing Curse.[77] Dumbledore makes this claim when he is telling Harry about the prophecy made concerning him: "There is a room in the Department of Mysteries . . . that is kept locked at all times. It contains a force that is at once more wonderful and more terrible than death, than human intelligence, than forces of nature."[78]

That is certainly a bold thing to say about love. This is one of the most fascinating themes in all of Harry Potter because it is not clear from everyday life that love is more powerful than every other force in the world, death included. Even marriage, the most abiding form of human love, ends with death ("till death do us part"). Is there really a love that is greater than death? Is there a love that endures beyond the grave?

The Bible teaches that there is. The climax of the Song of Songs, the great love poem, puts it this way:

> Place me like a seal over your heart,
>   like a seal on your arm;
> for love is as strong as death,
>   its jealousy unyielding as the grave.
> It burns like blazing fire,
>   like a mighty flame.
> Many waters cannot quench love;
>   rivers cannot sweep it away.
> If one were to give
>   all the wealth of one's house for love,
>   it would be utterly scorned. (8:6–7)

The line "like a mighty flame" could also be translated "like the very flame of the LORD," and thus, the poem is hinting that the love that is as strong as death is the very love of God. In Jesus Christ we see just what this means. This is one of the themes in Harry Potter where the connection to the Bible is especially clear because of how much the Bible says about the love, sacrifice, and even blood of Jesus. He is like Lily in many ways. The apostle John says, "This is how we know what love is: Jesus Christ laid down his life for us" (1 John 3:16). Jesus' sacrifice on the cross is the epitome of his love, and his shed blood then gives lasting protection to his people.

One of the images that gets used again and again for Jesus is that of the Passover Lamb, which is a reference back to the exodus of the Israelites from slavery in Egypt. After sending nine different plagues on the Egyptians, God was going to send one more: the firstborn male of every household was going to be killed. The Israelites, however, were told that if they took the blood of a lamb and painted it over the doorframe of their homes, they would be spared. The blood was a refuge for those inside.

Jesus understood the same thing to be happening with his blood that was shed on the cross. Indeed, Jesus timed his final confrontation with the Jewish and Roman authorities (which he knew would lead to his death) with the Passover Festival.[79] During the Passover meal that he had with his disciples on the night before he was crucified, Jesus took a cup and said, "This is my blood of the covenant, which is poured out for many for the forgiveness of sins" (Matthew 26:28). It is a picture of the love of God, of the great lengths that he is willing to go to rescue his people—to the point of shedding his own blood for them.

And by pouring out his blood, Jesus secured the forgiveness of sins. The Bible teaches that all people have sinned by worshiping idols, and by doing so they have rejected God and cut themselves off from the source of life. The consequence of this is death. But by shedding his blood, Jesus took upon himself the punishment for sin that would otherwise fall on them. The apostle Paul says, "God sent his own son in the likeness of sinful flesh, and as a sin-offering; and, right there in the flesh, he condemned sin" (Romans 8:3 NTfE). Because Jesus took the condemnation for sin upon himself, sins are forgiven and consequently death loses its power. The blood of Jesus becomes a refuge that not even death can penetrate.

The glorious proof of this is that Jesus has been raised from the dead. Paul says it this way: "For we know that since Christ was raised from the dead, he cannot die again; death no longer has mastery over him. The death he died, he died to sin once for all; but the life he lives, he lives to God" (Romans 6:9–10). The resurrection of Jesus is the sign that death has been defeated, and through faith in him, we can share in his life. His blood in us (represented as we drink the cup in the Lord's Supper) tethers us to life—his resurrection life.

Here, then, we have a self-sacrificial love that is more powerful than death because it defeats death and endures forever. As Paul says triumphantly, "For I am convinced that neither *death* nor life, neither angels nor demons, neither the present nor the future, nor any powers, neither height nor depth, nor anything else in all creation will be able to separate us from the love of God that is in Christ Jesus our Lord" (Romans 8:38–39).

Lily's sacrificial love not only places protection around Harry, though; it also transforms him internally. Dumbledore is always clear that Harry's greatest strength is his capacity to love, so it is fitting that the whole story ends much the same way it begins—with self-sacrificial love that gives magical protection.

When Harry looks into Snape's memories at the end of the seventh book, he witnesses an important exchange where Dumbledore tells Snape that a part of Voldemort's soul lives inside Harry and that Harry must die in order for Voldemort to die. Snape is horrified by this and accuses Dumbledore of raising Harry like a "pig for slaughter."[80] Very interestingly, a similar metaphor is used in a prophecy about Jesus: he is to be "led like a lamb to the slaughter" (Isaiah 53:7). Just as Lily died for her son to protect him, so now Harry must die for his friends to protect them. He taps into the same deep magic Lily did, so that when he returns and the final battle happens, Voldemort's curses do not work properly on Harry's friends. The same love that he received he gave to others.

The Bible says the same thing about Christians: "We love because he first loved us" (1 John 4:19). It is through knowing and experiencing the love of Jesus for us that we become people who are characterized by love. Or as Paul says, "For the Messiah's love makes us press on. We have come to the conviction that one died for all, and therefore all died. And he died for all in order that those who live should live no longer for themselves, but for him who died and was raised on their behalf" (2 Corinthians 5:14–15 NTfE). When we see the sacrifice Jesus made for us on the cross, we are moved in our hearts to love others and lay down our lives for them. And therefore, the Bible teaches that the love of Christ not only conquers death and protects us from the greatest threat that stands against us, it is the deep magic that saves us from our selfishness so that we might be free to love—the very thing we were made for.

9

Dumbledore

Has it not occurred to you, my poor puffed-up popinjay, that there might be an excellent reason why the headmaster of Hogwarts is not confiding every tiny detail of his plans to you?

—PHINEAS NIGELLUS[81]

ONE FEATURE THAT MAKES Harry Potter a riveting read is that the intricacy and intensity of the story evolve as Harry, Ron, and Hermione grow up. But even by the seventh book, the three are still just seventeen years old—yet they shoulder the burden of the entire wizarding world. Of course, they get a lot of help from older witches and wizards along the way, most notably from Dumbledore, the mastermind and leader of those who resist Voldemort and the Death Eaters. But it is surprising how hands-off Dumbledore is in the help he provides Harry, Ron, and Hermione. Some might even call him crazy for entrusting the fate of the wizarding world to three teenagers while giving them such limited information. But in the end, Dumbledore's elusive approach proves his brilliance.

We first see Dumbledore's propensity for providing limited information in the first book when Harry, Ron, and Hermione are reflecting together in the hospital wing after the Sorcerer's Stone has been destroyed. Ron asks Harry if he thinks Dumbledore intended for Harry to go through the trapdoor to keep the Stone from getting into the wrong hands. It was, after all, Dumbledore who sent Harry his father's Invisibility Cloak as a Christmas present. Hermione interjects that she thinks that would be a horrible thing for Dumbledore to do because Harry could have been killed. But Harry disagrees: "No it isn't. . . . I think he knows more or less everything that goes on here, you know. I reckon he had a pretty good idea we were going to try, and instead of stopping us, he just taught us enough to help."[82]

Again, in the third book, Dumbledore entrusts a very important task to Harry and Hermione (Ron is lying in bed with a broken leg). Sirius Black is locked in a room on the seventh floor, and dementors are about to be brought in to administer the Kiss on him. Dumbledore is unable to persuade anyone of Sirius's innocence, so he asks Harry and Hermione to rescue him. But remarkably, he does not tell them exactly how they should do it. Instead, he says, "If all goes well, you will be able to save more than one innocent life tonight"—meaning that he intends for them to use the Hippogriff Buckbeak to save Sirius.[83] But he does not tell them that explicitly! With such high stakes, it is shocking that he leaves them to figure it out on their own.

And finally, in the seventh book, Dumbledore gives the trio one final test as they set out on their quest to destroy Horcruxes. He leaves them mysterious objects in his will, but he does not explain the significance of these objects and leaves them to work it out on their own. Though Dumbledore did not know exactly when he would die, he did know that it would happen within a year of putting on Marvolo Gaunt's ring. Thus, there would have been plenty of time to share with them why he would give them these objects. It seems that Dumbledore is leaving a lot to chance when the stakes could not be higher, but it must be that one of the reasons Dumbledore tests Harry, Ron, and Hermione is that he *trusts* them. He trusts that they, particularly Harry, will be able to figure out what he has left them to do. Dumbledore makes this very clear in his final words to Kingsley and Lupin that demonstrate the faith he placed in Harry: "Harry is the best hope we have. Trust him."[84]

The point of Dumbledore's testing, then, is not to see if they will succeed or not—he has already placed his trust in them—but to help the trio, and especially Harry, on their quest. There is something to be gained by not disclosing information immediately and letting Harry, Ron, and Hermione figure things out. There is a growth process to be undergone, which otherwise would be stunted if they were told everything they wanted to know.

And of course, it drives them crazy. Ron is so infuriated by the lack of guidance that he leaves. And while Harry stays the course, he begins to lose faith in Dumbledore. This reaches a breaking point after the near escape from Godric's Hollow when Harry reads a chapter of Rita Skeeter's *The Life and Lies of Albus Dumbledore* and learns damning things about Dumbledore's family history and his friendship with Gellert Grindelwald—things Dumbledore never told him. Harry explodes in anger that Dumbledore asked him to put his life on the line again and again but never trusted him enough to confide in him. Hermione maintains that Dumbledore changed and that he really did love Harry, but Harry cannot believe this: "This isn't love, the mess he's left me in."[85]

Ouch. At this point, all trust has been broken. The withholding of knowledge has led Harry to believe that there is no way Dumbledore could have loved him. How can you love someone whom you leave them in the dark?

But not long after this, Harry begins to have a change of heart. While burying Dobby at Shell Cottage, he reflects on some of the things he has just witnessed that have justified Dumbledore's wisdom: Ron's Deluminator was perfectly suited to help him rejoin the quest, and Wormtail's magical hand ended up killing him like Dumbledore had hinted at. And Harry wonders if Dumbledore knew more than he was letting on. Perhaps Dumbledore knew what he was doing in only providing clues to the Deathly Hallows but no clear details. Perhaps Dumbledore had good reasons for leaving Harry, Ron, and Hermione in the dark and forcing them to work things out. Harry's trust in his headmaster begins to return and he chooses to hunt Horcruxes again despite not knowing everything he wishes he did.[86]

And Dumbledore, for his part, does have good reasons for withholding information from Harry. When disclosing to Snape that he would be the one to tell Harry that Harry must eventually be killed by Voldemort, he tells Snape to wait until Voldemort begins to fiercely protect Nagini. The information must be withheld until then because, if not, "how could he have the strength to do what must be done?"[87] Thus, one reason Dumbledore withholds information from Harry is that he would not be able to handle it. If he knew that he was going to have to be killed, he would not have been able to complete the mission of destroying Horcruxes. It would have been too overwhelming for him.

He also explains another piece of his reasoning to Harry during their reunion in King's Cross Station at the end of the seventh book. Harry asks why Dumbledore had to make things so difficult, to which Dumbledore responds, "I'm afraid I counted on Miss Granger to slow you up."[88] In other words, he was relying on Hermione's cool thinking to balance out Harry's tendency towards impulsiveness. He wanted to force the trio to take the time to figure out the significance of the Deathly Hallows so that, should they come to possess them, they would use them wisely.

In summary, then, Dumbledore withholds information from Harry for two reasons. First, some information, such as the fact that Harry must let himself be killed, would be too overwhelming for him if he was told up front. And second, other information, such as insight into the Deathly Hallows, needed to be worked out over time to give space for Harry's understanding to be shaped so that he would not take the Hallows selfishly. Dumbledore thought the waiting and the struggle would purify Harry's motivations. And Dumbledore's testing is, of course, vindicated because when Harry finally does get all this information, he is prepared and has been formed into a person who has the strength to face Voldemort.

This theme of testing is one that can be found throughout the pages of the Bible. And perhaps the most famous story of testing is one that happens at the end of the life of Abraham, the father of Israel. Abraham has walked with God throughout his life, but he has also failed at various times and known God to be patient with him.

And now the story says, "Some time later God tested Abraham" (Genesis 22:1). The crucial thing to note here is that this testing takes place at the end of Abraham's life, after his character has been shaped and formed. God only tests him because he knows that at this point in his life, Abraham has the capacity to succeed. God trusts him, as it were.

And this is Abraham's test: he must take his son Isaac to Mount Moriah and offer him as a sacrifice to God. Isaac was Abraham's most precious son—the one who was promised to him when his wife Sarah was unable to bear children and who was to be the child through whom a great nation would come. This request raises plenty of issues that have been widely debated. Examples include: How is it that God can command someone to murder an innocent human being? Isn't that evil? Should a person obey God when he is calling them to do something that they know to be wrong? Space does not allow an answer to those questions here, but it is noteworthy that God ultimately prevents Abraham from killing his son Isaac—though Abraham does not know that at the outset of his journey. The purpose is to test him.

While Abraham and Isaac go on the three-day journey to the mountain that God commands, Abraham had to be mulling over in his head what God had asked him to do: "Didn't God promise me that through Isaac he would make a great nation that will bless the world? How could that happen if he is dead?" In the end, Abraham reasons that if God has promised that Isaac will continue his line and that he has also commanded him to kill Isaac, it must be that God will find a way to still keep his promise, even if that means raising Isaac back from the dead (Hebrews 11:19). His faith was tested and formed while information was withheld from him. At the climax of the story, however, when Abraham raises his knife over his bound son, an angel calls out to Abraham and tells him not to touch the boy. Instead, Abraham finds a ram caught in a thicket on the mountain, and he sacrifices the ram instead.

We often find ourselves in similar situations to Harry's and Abraham's. Our lives are perplexing with no clear way forward, and it seems as if information is being withheld from us. We are confused and wonder if we can trust God. Or perhaps if there even is a God. I remember sharing some of my own struggles along these lines with a friend one time, and he had some very insightful words. He said that God only entrusts suffering to us to the point that we can bear it. In other words, if you have placed your faith in God and are suffering a particular pain in your life, it means that God trusts your character enough (that he has shaped in you by his Holy Spirit!) for you to persevere through it. And there is hope in that.

The apostle Paul writes, "No temptation [or trial[89]] has overtaken you except what is common to mankind. And God is faithful; he will not let you be tempted beyond what you can bear. But when you are tempted, he will also provide a way out so that you can endure it" (1 Corinthians 10:13). What this means is that information that may seem important at the time—like *how* we will make it through a trial, or *when* it will end—is not good for us to know. Instead, in the waiting we are called to endure, knowing that we are being refined by the pain like gold is refined by fire (1 Peter 1:7).

Just as Harry grew to trust Dumbledore anew by reflecting on the way Dumbledore had *provided* for them (in his will and in other ways), so our trust grows the same way. At the end of the story of Abraham and Isaac, Abraham names the mountain "The LORD Will Provide," because God had provided a ram to replace his son (Genesis 22:14). But one of the core teachings of Christianity is that God has provided *his* only Son, Jesus Christ, as a sacrifice for us—for him there was no replacement. So now, when we are tempted to doubt God's love because he tests us and withholds information from us, we can look back to the crucifixion of Jesus and say, just as God said to Abraham, "Now I know that you [love me], because you have not withheld from me your son, your only son" (Genesis 22:12).[90] Or as the apostle Paul says, "He who did not spare his own Son, but gave him up for us all—how will he not also, along with him, graciously give us all things?" (Romans 8:32).

10

Dobby

Harry Potter freed Dobby! . . . Harry Potter set Dobby free!

—DOBBY[91]

ONE OF THE MOST memorable and widely-beloved characters in Harry Potter is Dobby. Dobby is a house-elf, a small and peculiar-looking creature who is "bound to serve one house and one family forever."[92] There is only one way a house-elf can be freed from this bondage: his master must give him clothes. Thus, the rags house-elves wear are not just a sign of their poverty—they are a sign of their slavery and humiliation.

When we first meet Dobby in the second book, he is serving the Malfoy family, though we do not know it at the time. He appears in Harry's bedroom to try to keep Harry from returning to Hogwarts because he is aware of Lucius Malfoy's plan to reopen the Chamber of Secrets. And since Dobby's warning is something the Malfoys would disapprove of, Dobby must punish himself for it. Indeed, Dobby must punish himself any time he even speaks ill of the Malfoys by doing things like banging his head against the wall or shutting his ears in the oven door. It is a brutal life that Dobby lives, and it is conditions like these that ultimately lead Hermione to start S.P.E.W. and fight for house-elf rights.

After a couple more attempts to keep Harry away from Hogwarts, Dobby disappears from the narrative for a while, but he reappears for what becomes the turning point in his life. When Harry returns from his trip into the Chamber of Secrets and is reflecting on it with Dumbledore, Lucius Malfoy shows up with Dobby. And on a whim, Harry comes up with a plan to free him: he wraps Tom Riddle's diary in one of his socks and gives it to Lucius Malfoy. Consequently, when Lucius rips the sock off, Dobby catches it—and since a sock is an article of clothing, Dobby is freed.

Dobby is ecstatic over his newfound freedom and deeply grateful to Harry, and in the books that follow he tries to help Harry in any way he can. He gets Christmas gifts for Harry. He gets a job at Hogwarts. He wakes Harry up just in time for the second task of the Triwizard Tournament and gives him gillyweed so that he can breathe underwater. He tells Harry about the Room of Requirement so that Dumbledore's Army can have a place to practice defensive magic. He warns Harry when Dolores Umbridge finds out about D.A. meetings. And he follows Draco around to find out what he is up to when Harry observes him doing suspicious things.

It is after this last task that we learn that Dobby struggles with his newfound freedom at times. When giving Harry his report on Draco, which requires that he speak negatively of him, Dobby attempts to jump into the fire as a self-punishment. Harry prevents him from doing so—and Dobby comes to his senses—but it is as if he still feels enslaved to the Malfoys sometimes. The years of slavery have left an imprint on his mind and body that has not been broken overnight.

Dobby's motivation to do all these things for Harry is because, as he says, "Dobby wishes he could help Harry Potter, for Harry Potter set Dobby free."[93] It is quite remarkable—Dobby shows even more devotion to Harry as a free elf than he ever did to the Malfoys when he was their servant. Indeed, we might think from how loyal he is to Harry that he has become *Harry's* house-elf. But he has not—he is free. He is a free elf who serves the one who freed him.

And we see the full extent of Dobby's devotion to Harry in the final book when he rescues Harry and his friends from Malfoy Manor. Before Dobby shows up, it appears as if all is lost: Harry and Ron are wandless; Hermione is borderline unconscious; and Voldemort is just seconds away from being close enough to Apparate to the house. Moreover, Malfoy Manor is the home of Dobby's former masters. After suffering brutal treatment at the Malfoy's hands for years and experiencing post-traumatic stress in the time since his liberation, merely setting foot in that house would have been nerve-racking.

But Dobby summons the courage. He magically unscrews the chandelier and disarms Narcissa Malfoy, creating an opportunity for Harry, Ron, Hermione, and Griphook to gather into groups and Disapparate. Bellatrix shrieks that Dobby has defied his master, but Dobby, trembling a bit, declares triumphantly that he has no master. While he is Disapparating, though, Bellatrix throws her knife and it pierces his chest. As soon as they arrive at Shell Cottage, the elf sways, falls into Harry's arms, and dies; it is one of the most heart-wrenching moments in the whole series. In tribute to him, Harry digs his grave by hand, and the inscription Harry writes on his tombstone is perfect because it highlights Dobby's most defining attribute: "HERE LIES DOBBY, A FREE ELF."[94]

Dobby's story gives a very illuminating perspective on what freedom is. Charles Taylor, a Catholic philosopher, has noted that many people influenced by Western culture think of freedom as "negative freedom," or freedom from any and all constraints.[95] We might call this a "freedom from . . ." Freedom from authority. Freedom from rules. Freedom from oppression.

But the freedom Dobby experiences is so much more than that. Yes, it includes being set free from his cruel masters, but Dobby's freedom also entails love and service. Many people can relate to this experience. If you asked most people when it is that they feel most free, they would likely say that it is "when they are truly loved and loving another."[96] It is in the context of love that we tend to feel the most ourselves and the most alive. And this is an idea that is found in the Bible as well.

Early in the Bible we meet a group of people who are in the same condition as Dobby: slavery to a cruel master. They are the Israelites, and they were enslaved by the Egyptians for over four hundred years. The Egyptians subjected them to hard labor and treated them brutally, even killing their baby boys to limit the growth of their population. But the Bible also teaches that all humans, whether they know it or not, are living in slavery to a cruel master—only in this case, the slavery is a result of their own choices. Jesus calls this slave-master Sin: "Everyone who sins is a slave to sin" (John 8:34). Referring back to chapter 3 on the Mirror of Erised, we all worship and serve idols that, because they are not the Creator, suck the life from us and enslave us (Romans 1:25). And this makes for a miserable existence.

But Jesus also said that he came to set people free from this slavery: "So if the Son sets you free, you will be free indeed" (John 8:36). He did this chiefly through dying on the cross. By his crucifixion, Jesus took the full weight of our sin upon himself so that we could be forgiven, and this "disarmed the rulers and authorities"—including the idols—that enslaved us, thus freeing us from them (Colossians 2:13–15).

But freedom in the Bible does not simply mean the freedom to do whatever we want. Instead, like Dobby, freedom entails loving and serving the one who set us free. This is why God tells Moses, the great Israelite prophet who led his people out of slavery in Egypt, to say to Pharaoh again and again, "Let my people go, *so that they may worship me* in the wilderness" (Exodus 7:16). This is what redemption is all about! (The word "redemption" is a word taken from the slave market to describe what happens when a person buys a slave and sets them free.) The whole point of the Israelites being set free from slavery in Egypt was so that they could worship God, the one who set them free. Merely being set free from slavery is not true freedom—true freedom is found in love and devotion.

And this devotion should be so strong that it looks like slavery to a new master. The apostle Paul puts it this way: "But now that you have been set free from sin and have become *slaves* of God, the benefit you reap leads to holiness, and the result is eternal life" (Romans 6:22). He says that we are simultaneously enslaved and free. This worship and devotion to God might look like slavery, but it does not feel like it because it is motivated by love, not fear. "Perfect love casts out fear" (1 John 4:18). This is true freedom. Simply put, it is the world of difference, as Dobby shows us, between serving the Malfoys and serving Harry.

More specifically, the Bible teaches that this devotion to God will be lived out by loving other people. As the apostle Paul says, "You, my brothers and sisters, were called to be free. But do not use your freedom to indulge the flesh; rather, serve one another humbly in love" (Galatians 5:13). In other words, just because you have been granted freedom, do not simply do whatever you please. We might call this a "freedom to . . ." Freedom to love. Freedom to serve. Freedom to play a meaningful role in the lives of others. You will be most free when you are worshiping God and serving other people in love. It is what you were made to do. And therefore, the story of Dobby—struggling at times to remember he is free but mostly living to love and serve the one who freed him—is a beautiful picture of what freedom really is.

11

Fawkes

*And then an unearthly and beautiful sound filled the air. . . . It
was the sound of hope to Harry.*

—Phoenix song in the Little Hangleton graveyard[97]

Critics, and even casual observers, have long identified so-
called "Christ figures" in various works of literature and film. The
Christ figure is a "literary technique that the author uses to draw
allusions between their characters and the biblical Jesus."[98] By
evoking the widely-admired story of Jesus Christ, authors impart
deeper significance to their characters. Intriguingly, there are actually a number of different Christ figures in Harry Potter. Certainly
Harry himself has the clearest resemblance to Jesus, as we will see
in a later chapter, but there are a number of other characters in the
story who also echo the story of Jesus. And one of them is not even
a human—it is Fawkes the phoenix.

We first meet Fawkes in the second book when Harry, already
feeling anxious because he had been spotted at the scene where the
Basilisk attacked, witnesses the phoenix burst into flames and die
in Dumbledore's office. He is understandably shocked and frightened by this, but when Dumbledore enters, he is very pleased and
explains to Harry that Fawkes, as a phoenix, regularly dies and
is reborn from the ashes. He also tells Harry that phoenixes have

two other special abilities and one defining virtue: "They can carry immensely heavy loads, their tears have healing powers, and they make highly *faithful* pets."[99]

Harry witnesses the full gamut of Fawkes's prowess while in the Chamber of Secrets. First, the phoenix's sudden appearance in the deepest recesses of the castle is a testament to how faithful he is to Dumbledore. As the headmaster says to Harry, "You must have shown me real loyalty down in the Chamber. Nothing but that could have called Fawkes to you."[100] Furthermore, when the Basilisk's fang pierces Harry's arm, injecting its deadly venom, Fawkes begins to weep. He lets his tears drip on the wound so that when Harry looks down at his arm, "a pearly patch of tears was shining all around the wound—except that there *was* no wound."[101] The tears had healed it. And finally, to ascend the pipe leading out of the Chamber of Secrets, Fawkes carries four humans—Harry, Ron, Ginny, and Gilderoy Lockhart—back up to the school, which is quite a feat for a bird.

Fawkes's two special abilities seem totally unrelated; but upon a closer look, there is a deeper connection between them. Quite literally, phoenixes can carry heavy physical loads and bring physical healing, but as the story goes on, it becomes clear that phoenixes can carry immensely heavy emotional burdens and bring emotional healing as well. This happens through the exquisite phoenix song.

Harry first hears this song when he is in dire straits in the Chamber of Secrets facing Tom Riddle and the Basilisk without his wand. Ginny is slowly dying, and it seems like there is no hope of rescue. But at that moment, he begins to hear music:

> It was eerie, spine-tingling, unearthly; it lifted the hair on Harry's scalp and made his heart feel as though it was swelling to twice its normal size. Then, as the music reached such a pitch that Harry felt it vibrating inside his own ribs, flames erupted at the top of the nearest pillar. A crimson bird the size of a swan had appeared, piping its weird music to the vaulted ceiling.[102]

The phoenix song sparked courage in Harry. It was able to, in some sense, help carry his burden of fear. A similar thing happens when Harry is facing Voldemort in the Little Hangleton graveyard. This is the most traumatic moment of Harry's life up to this point as he watches Cedric be murdered, Voldemort resurrect, and the Death Eaters jeer; and he believes his own death is imminent. But when Voldemort and Harry fire their spells at each other, their wands connect, producing a golden cage of light, and phoenix song begins to emanate from the threads: "It was the sound of hope to Harry . . . the most beautiful and welcome thing he had ever heard in his life. . . . He felt as though the song were inside him instead of just around him. . . . It was the song he connected with Dumbledore."[103] Presumably, this happens because the core of each of their wands is a phoenix tail feather from Fawkes. The song invigorates Harry so that he has the strength to hold the connection.

And finally, at the end of the sixth book, we hear phoenix song once more. Except this time the song is different—it is a lament. Dumbledore has just been murdered, and everyone in the hospital wing is in utter shock. They are feeling deep sorrow at having lost Dumbledore, whom they each loved and admired. And their cause is looking bleak. While Dumbledore was alive, the prospect of facing Voldemort and his followers felt more hopeful because they always knew they had "the only one he ever feared" on their side, no matter how bad things looked.[104] But now he is gone. The room is filled with palpable grief and despair, and a few people are crying. But then, they hear music:

> Somewhere out in the darkness, a phoenix was singing in a way Harry had never heard before: a stricken lament of terrible beauty. . . . It was his own grief turned magically to song that echoed across the grounds and through the castle windows. How long they all stood there, listening, he did not know, nor why it seemed to ease their pain a little to listen to the sound of their mourning.[105]

Here we see phoenix tears—expressed in song—carrying the heavy burden of grief and healing the pain of loss. Thus, we should not be surprised that a phoenix has the special ability to both carry heavy loads and heal with its tears—these powers belong together.

Brené Brown is a professor who researches vulnerability and empathy, and her studies show that people in deep distress do not primarily need someone to fix their problems—they need connection. They need empathy. They need someone to "feel with" them. And the only way that happens is when the empathizing person "connects with something in themselves that knows that feeling [of deep distress]."[106] They have to reflect on a past experience in their own life that produced similarly painful emotions so that they can feel the other person's hurt and connect with them. It is tears of empathy that have the power to lift other people's burdens.

The Bible attests to this as well. One of the commands given to Christians is to "carry each other's burdens, and in this way you will fulfill the law of Christ" (Galatians 6:2). Christians are to be a family who love each other by carrying each other's burdens, much like the story of the paralytic man whose four friends carried him to Jesus because he could not walk (Mark 2:1–11). Another command given to Christians is to "weep with those who weep" (Romans 12:15). Jesus himself practiced this after the death of his friend Lazarus (John 11:1–45). Even though he knew he would raise Lazarus from the dead, when Jesus was led to Lazarus's tomb and saw his friends crying, he wept with them and shared their grief (though certainly Jesus was feeling grief himself because Lazarus was his friend as well). The point is that one of the chief ways Christians carry one another's burdens is through their tears—through entering into and feeling each other's pain, which often manifests itself in praying for each other.

To that end, the Bible has another resource that has the power to lift a person's burdens: the Psalms. The Psalms are the recorded songs and prayers of God's people, and they lyricize the whole gamut of human emotions, including fear, grief, anger, shame, longing, despair, confusion, gratitude, and joy. However, when the Psalms are broken down by type, the largest category is that of lament—that is, those that are expressing distressing emotions. Many of these psalms come from a place of heavy sorrow and a constant flow of tears: "I am worn out from my groaning. All night long I flood my bed with weeping and drench my couch with tears" (Psalm 6:6). "My tears have been my food day and night" (Psalm 42:3) "Record my misery; list my tears on your scroll" (Psalm 56:8).

There is something fitting about this emphasis on lament. As we taste life's bitter afflictions—what King David calls "[walking] through the valley of the shadow of death"—it is consoling to read the prayers and songs of others who have walked that valley before us and put their tears into words, especially when we do not know what to pray ourselves (Psalm 23:4 ESV). As one pastor has said, the Psalms are a "medicine chest for the heart."[107] Indeed, these songs, as the phoenix song, enter inside of us as we pray them, and as we hear our "own grief turned magically to song," they ease our pain a little as we listen to the sound of our mourning.[108] Faithful believers have been praying these prayers regularly for millennia, and believers today would benefit from incorporating them into our lives and worship services and find that they have healing power.

While the tears of our brothers and sisters and the tears of the Psalms can help lift our burdens and heal our pain, there is only one person in the Bible whose tears bring permanent healing: Jesus Christ. During his ministry, it is clear that Jesus knew where it was all heading, and in the hours before he was crucified, there is an account that opens a window into his heart and mind as he faced his impending death. It is a view of the calm before the storm, but the storm is already beginning to rage inside Jesus because he knows just how perilous the winds and the rain will get.

He took a few of his closest disciples with him to a garden called Gethsemane and poured out his heart to them: "My soul is overwhelmed with sorrow to the point of death" (Mark 14:34). In other words, "My sorrow is so great that it could kill me." Another account indicates that he was in so much agony that he was sweating drops of blood (Luke 22:44). His mind and body in travail, Jesus prayed that the harrowing suffering he was about to undergo would be stopped. And when he did so, he prayed with "fervent cries and *tears* to the one who could save him from death" (Hebrews 5:7). Tears of anguish. Tears of desperation. A bodily indicator of how badly he wanted to avoid the abyss he was walking into. But as he prays, he accepts that his crucifixion is the only way to bring salvation and life to the world—and thus he submits to it.

In hindsight, then, we see that these tears shed by Jesus in the garden of Gethsemane are healing tears. They are an antidote not to Basilisk venom but to the venomous destruction that the ancient serpent has unleashed upon the world (Genesis 3). They are the tears to end all tears. Because Jesus shed these tears and suffered on the cross, he healed the world once and for all, such that a day is coming when God will "wipe every tear from their eyes. There will be no more death or mourning or crying or pain, for the old order of things has passed away" (Revelation 21:4). Death is absent from this new world because "death has been swallowed up in victory" (1 Corinthians 15:54). Just as Fawkes swallowed Voldemort's Killing Curse when it was heading for Dumbledore during their duel in the Ministry of Magic Atrium, so Jesus swallowed the curse of sin when he was crucified. And therefore, because Jesus wept, we know that one day we will weep no more. "By his wounds we are healed" (Isaiah 53:5). Jesus is the true phoenix who dies and rises again from the ashes to bring healing to the world.

12

The Marauders

I doubt whether any Hogwarts students ever found out more about the Hogwarts grounds and Hogsmeade than we did. . . . And that's how we came to write the Marauder's Map, and sign it with our nicknames.

—REMUS LUPIN[109]

ONE OF THE BRANCHES of magic that Hogwarts students must learn is Transfiguration, and witches and wizards who have mastered an especially advanced form of Transfiguration—the ability to transform into animals—are called Animagi. Unlike normal Transfiguration, which happens by spell, an Animagus can turn into an animal at will. But the process of becoming an Animagus is notoriously long and complex. It is so arduous, in fact, that there are only seven known Animagi registered with the Ministry of Magic. One of them is Minerva McGonagall, who has the ability to transform into a cat. However, there are other Animagi who are not registered with the Ministry of Magic, such as Rita Skeeter, who has the ability to transform into a beetle so that she can sneak around and eavesdrop on conversations. But we also learn about three others.

Remus Lupin tells the story. At a young age, Lupin was bit by a werewolf and became one himself. This brought a double affliction: There was the painful transformation itself that would have caused a young boy great anxiety in the days leading up to full moon each month. But there was also the shame and isolation that came along with being perceived as dangerous—which, of course, was true, but only during the full moon. Given his condition, it seemed like there was no way Lupin would be able to attend Hogwarts since his presence would put other students at risk of being bitten by him. However, Dumbledore became the headmaster of Hogwarts, and he came up with a plan that would enable Lupin to attend school: Lupin would be taken to the Shrieking Shack each month just before he transformed, and the Whomping Willow would be planted to keep people away.

As Lupin describes it, his transformations were especially awful because, since he did not have humans to bite, he bit himself. But, for the first time in his life, he had friends: James Potter, Sirius Black, and Peter Pettigrew. He tried desperately to keep his secret from them because he was afraid they would not want to be his friends if they found out what he was, and he made up excuses as to why he had to go away each month. But eventually they figured it out. However, instead of deserting him and treating him as an outcast like the rest of society had done, they did something quite extraordinary—they became Animagi. Lupin explains to Harry,

> It took them the best part of three years to work out how to do it. Your father and Sirius here were the cleverest students in the school, and lucky they were, because the Animagus transformation can go horribly wrong—one reason the Ministry keeps a close watch on those attempting to do it. . . . Finally, in our fifth year, they managed it. They could each turn into a different animal at will. . . . They couldn't keep me company as humans, so they kept me company as animals. . . . They sneaked out of the castle every month under James's Invisibility Cloak. They transformed. . . . Under their influence, I became less dangerous. My body was still wolfish, but my mind seemed to become less so while I was with them.[110]

That is a remarkable thing to do for a friend. James, Sirius, and Peter not only stick by Lupin—at great cost to themselves they transform to become like him. They take the risk of trying the Animagus transformation unsupervised and take on the form of animals so that they can be with their friend in his hour of need each month. And the result is that Lupin's transformations become, as he says, "not only bearable, but the best times of my life."[111]

In many ways, the Animagus transformation that James, Sirius, and Peter undergo for their friend echoes one of the key beliefs of Christianity: the incarnation. The incarnation is the teaching that God entered our world by taking on human flesh in the person of Jesus of Nazareth. In the Old Testament, God's presence dwelled on earth in the temple in Jerusalem; it was manifest as a cloud that filled the temple and reminded worshipers that God was there (1 Kings 8:10–11). At a later point in Israel's history, the prophet Ezekiel had a vision of the presence of God departing the temple because of Israel's rebellion (Ezekiel 10–11). God could no longer put up with their wickedness, and thus he left them to be exiled and the temple was destroyed. But not without a promise: God said that one day he would return to Israel and restore the temple.

Christians believe Jesus is the fulfillment of this promise. During his ministry, Jesus referred to *himself* as the temple, the embodiment of God's presence (John 2:19–22). This is what we celebrate at Christmas—that the author of life was born of a woman to redeem humanity and restore this world to the way it was meant to be. The apostle Paul captures it beautifully in a poem:

> [Christ Jesus], being in very nature God,
>   did not consider equality with God something to be used to
> his own advantage;
> rather, he made himself nothing
>   by taking the very nature of a servant,
>   being made in human likeness.
> And being found in appearance as a man,
>   he humbled himself
>   by becoming obedient to death—
>   even death on a cross!
> Therefore God exalted him to the highest place

and gave him the name that is above every name,
that at the name of Jesus every knee should bow,
    in heaven and on earth and under the earth,
and every tongue acknowledge that Jesus Christ is Lord,
    to the glory of God the Father. (Philippians 2:6–11)

Just as James, Sirius, and Peter, though they were humans, took on the form of animals to identify with their friend and help him in his misery, so Jesus, though he was God, took on the form of a human to identify with humanity and help us in our misery. And just like the Animagus transformation, it came at a great cost to him—to the point of dying an excruciating and humiliating death on a cross. That is the very heart of the poem, and indeed it is the very heart of our faith.

One of the objections that people often raise to Christianity is the problem of evil: How can an all-good and all-powerful God allow suffering? If God is so good, and if he is powerful enough to prevent evil, why does he not simply put an end to it? This is a weighty question. It is often not just philosophical—we have all been hurt by this broken world in which suffering and evil seem to run rampant, and there are countless more stories of unspeakable pain that we hear about, read about, or see with our own eyes. Many of us have visceral reactions to these horrors, and it is only natural to ask, "Why?" Many people have rejected God because of this problem, and many believers struggle with it as well. When we take this problem to the Bible, we do not get a satisfactory answer—it does not answer all our questions. But we do get something else. The Anglican priest John Stott says it well:

> I could never myself believe in God, if it were not for the cross. The only God I believe in is the One Nietzsche ridiculed as "God on the cross." In the real world of pain, how could one worship a God who was immune to it? I have entered many Buddhist temples in different Asian countries and stood respectfully before the statue of the Buddha, his legs crossed, arms folded, eyes closed, the ghost of a smile playing round his mouth, a remote look on his face, detached from the agonies of the world. But each time after a while I have had to turn away. And in

imagination I have turned instead to that lonely, twisted, tortured figure on the cross, nails through hands and feet, back lacerated, limbs wrenched, brow bleeding from thorn-pricks, mouth dry and intolerably thirsty, plunged in Godforsaken darkness. That is the God for me! He laid aside his immunity to pain. He entered our world of flesh and blood, tears and death. He suffered for us. Our sufferings become more manageable in the light of his. There is still a question mark against human suffering, but over it we boldly stamp another mark, the cross that symbolizes divine suffering.[112]

Even if we do not get an answer as to why God allows suffering and evil, the message of the incarnation is that God has personally entered this world and experienced the very worst of it himself. He did so because of his love for us so that he could empathize with our often painful experience in this world. But he also became a human so that he could bear in his body the consequences of sin and die in our place to bring redemption and restoration to all of creation. Thus, the message of the Bible is that God really *has done* and *is doing* something about the evil in the world, and this happens preeminently through taking the full weight of evil upon himself in Jesus.

And unlike an Animagus, who transforms back and forth into an animal at will, Jesus became a human for good, and the Bible teaches that he is now sitting at the right hand of God in a glorified, resurrected human body (1 Corinthians 15:12–58). He is the true "image of the invisible God" who renews the image of God in humanity (Colossians 1:15). And when he returns, he will "transform our lowly body to be like his glorious body" so that our human condition will one day be not just bearable but a better life than we could ever imagine (Philippians 3:21 ESV).

13

Voldemort

*I fashioned myself a new name, a name I knew wizards
everywhere would one day fear to speak, when I had become
the greatest sorcerer in the world!*

—TOM RIDDLE[113]

CHARLES TAYLOR, ONE OF the world's leading thinkers on what it
means to live in a contemporary secular society, describes Western culture as operating within an "immanent frame." This means
the default belief is that "the world is a completely natural order
without any supernatural"—an absence of the transcendent.[114] The
material world is all that there is, and there is nothing to come after
our present existence. It is this assumption that makes belief in an
afterlife (or in God, for that matter) very difficult for many.

Despite having its origins in secular, Western society, life after death is hinted at in a number of ways throughout the Harry
Potter series. After the Sorcerer's Stone is destroyed in the first
book, Harry comes to the shocking realization that this means
Nicholas Flamel and his wife have chosen to submit to death. But
Dumbledore tells Harry that, though it may be hard for him to
imagine, death is not just an end; it is also a beginning: "To the
well-organized mind, death is but the next great adventure."[115]

What this adventure entails is not clear, though. When Harry asks Dumbledore during their reunion at King's Cross Station where the train might take him if he chose not to go back to face Voldemort, Dumbledore simply says, "On."[116] At the same time, characters who have died appear again in ethereal ways, such as through the power of the Resurrection Stone or when *Priori Incantatem* happens between Harry's and Voldemort's wands. These examples, along with others, imply that even when a person's body is destroyed, their *soul* lives on and can even animate portraits that are painted in honor of them.

Alongside this notion that the soul lives on even after the body has died is the theme that death is not the worst thing that can happen to a person—damage to one's soul would be far worse. The Dementor's Kiss is one example of this. Remus Lupin explains to Harry: "[The Dementor's Kiss is] what dementors do to those they wish to destroy utterly. I suppose there must be some kind of mouth under there, because they clamp their jaws upon the mouth of the victim and—and suck out his soul."[117] Harry is shocked and asks Lupin if they can really kill a person, to which Lupin responds,

> Oh no. . . . Much worse than that. You can exist without your soul, you know, as long as your brain and heart are still working. But you'll have no sense of self anymore, no memory, no . . . anything. There's no chance at all of recovery. You'll just—exist. As an empty shell. And your soul is gone forever . . . lost.[118]

Dumbledore and Voldemort, however, disagree on the question of whether there is something worse than death. When they are dueling in the Ministry of Magic Atrium at the end of the fifth book, Voldemort recognizes that Dumbledore is not trying to kill him and mocks him for it. In response, Dumbledore says that death is not the only way to destroy a person, and he tells Voldemort, "Your failure to understand that there are things worse than death has always been your greatest weakness."[119]

This idea comes up again in the memory of the conversation that Horace Slughorn has with the young Tom Riddle about Horcruxes. After explaining that the creation of a Horcrux would require one to split their soul, Slughorn says that almost everyone would prefer death to such an existence. In other words, it would be better to die than to maim one's soul.[120] But Voldemort does not believe this to be the case, and he goes ahead with the creation of his Horcruxes.

At the end of the story, though, Voldemort is forced to reckon with an existence worse than death. This happens after Voldemort hits Harry with the Killing Curse and Harry winds up in King's Cross Station. While he and Dumbledore are talking, a repulsive creature keeps moaning and flailing on the ground. It looks like a child, but its body is mutilated and it appears to have been abandoned. Harry has a desire to help the creature, but Dumbledore says, "You cannot help. . . . There is no help possible."[121] At the end of their conversation, Dumbledore suggests to Harry that this creature is a part of Voldemort's soul and a picture of what will ultimately happen to Voldemort himself.[122] This is Voldemort's fate: when he dies, he will face struggle and anguish that cannot be helped because of the evil he has done.

This is certainly a sobering scene, and I think most readers rightly feel the weight of it; but at the same time, I doubt many readers feel that Voldemort's fate is too severe. And there are at least three reasons for this. First, Voldemort's agony is self-inflicted. He is experiencing the pain of having split his soul again and again through murdering people and making Horcruxes, and the creature that is lying in King's Cross Station is simply one broken fragment of his soul from this cruel process. Voldemort has brought this fate upon himself.

Second, Voldemort has had many opportunities to show remorse for the atrocities he has committed and avoid the coming torment. Dumbledore says as much when Voldemort comes to Hogwarts on the pretext of asking for a job. He recounts how he once set fire to the young Riddle's closet to force him to return the things he stole, and he tells Voldemort he wishes he could do the same thing again—anything to bring Voldemort to repentance.[123] Likewise, Harry offers him one final chance in the Great Hall just before Voldemort tries to kill him. As he reveals why Voldemort's doom is sure, he admonishes, "Try . . . Try for some remorse."[124] Right up to the end, Voldemort could have changed course and shown remorse, which would have begun the process of healing his soul and altered his destiny.[125]

And third, in the wake of the trail of blood, suffering, and grief that Voldemort has left behind him, there is a sense that what eventually happens to him really is just. The Brockdale Bridge disaster, the Muggle-born Registration Commission, cruelty towards Muggles and house-elves, gratuitous murders—Voldemort is the mastermind of it all. Harry reflects on this after hearing that Neville's parents were tortured into insanity: "It was Voldemort, Harry thought . . . it all came back to Voldemort. . . . He was the one who had torn these families apart, who had ruined all these lives."[126] Readers rightly want justice to be done on behalf of all those whom Voldemort has hurt.

As it turns out, the fate of Lord Voldemort has many similarities to the Christian doctrine of God's judgment. This is perhaps the most uncomfortable and controversial of all of the teachings in the Bible, and even many Christians wrestle with the severity of it. But it is striking that the Bible describes judgment in the same three ways that Voldemort experiences it in Harry Potter.

First, it is self-inflicted. When the apostle Paul describes God's judgment against the evil of humanity, he says three times that God "gave them over" to their sins (Romans 1:24–28). In other words, the judgment of God is that he lets humans experience the consequences of the things they have done, just as Voldemort's judgment is experiencing the pain of having split his soul through murder. "Whoever digs a hole and scoops it out falls into the pit they have made. The trouble they cause recoils on them; their violence comes down on their own heads" (Psalm 7:15–16). According to the Bible, evil has a self-destructive nature to it.

Second, judgment in the Bible is preceded by calls for remorse and repentance. The apostle Peter makes this clear: "[The Lord] is patient with you, not wanting anyone to perish, but everyone to come to repentance" (2 Peter 3:9). God went so far as to send his only Son to die to be reconciled with his enemies. And even when he was crucified, Jesus pleaded with those who killed him and prayed that they would repent saying, "Father, forgive them, for they do not know what they are doing" (Luke 23:34). But as theologian Miroslav Volf says, after exhausting all means of being reconciled with someone to no avail, you must exclude them, which is exactly what God does with those who show no remorse.[127]

And finally, in the end, God is just, and as such, he cannot leave evil unpunished. Abraham expresses this sentiment when he says to God, "Will not the Judge of all the earth do right?" (Genesis 18:25). Most of us resonate with this desire to see justice done in our world, and the Christian teaching is that God, the righteous judge, *will* one day establish justice on earth. That is why when Jesus returns, according to the Bible, he will do so as a conquering king on a white horse, and "with *justice* he judges and wages war" (Revelation 19:11). Judgment is the right and just response to evil.

Just like Harry Potter, the Bible teaches that there is something worse than death. One passage calls it "the second death," and Voldemort's fate is a vivid portrayal of it—it is a place of great anguish that cannot be helped (Revelation 20:14). Truly lifeless. A place without hope. But even as we see soberly, and perhaps with shocking realization, that evil must be punished this way, we must also remember that the judgment of evil is the only hope for those who are oppressed. This is why everyone breaks out in raucous celebration and feasting the moment that Voldemort is vanquished for good: the judgment of evil means that justice and peace can finally be restored. This is cause for rejoicing and singing. Peeves composes a fitting song to celebrate Voldemort's downfall (which is characteristically crass), but the psalmist puts it much more eloquently, inviting all of creation to join in the song:

> Say among the nations, "The LORD reigns."
>   The world is firmly established, it cannot be moved;
>   he will *judge* the peoples with equity.
> Let the heavens rejoice, let the earth be glad;
>   let the sea resound, and all that is in it.
> Let the fields be jubilant, and everything in them;

let all the trees of the forest sing for joy.
Let all creation rejoice before the LORD, for he comes,
he comes to *judge* the earth.
He will *judge* the world in righteousness
and the peoples in his faithfulness. (Psalm 96:10–13)

14

Snape

My word, Severus, that I shall never reveal the best of you? . . .
If you insist.

— ALBUS DUMBLEDORE[128]

SOME PEOPLE'S STORIES ARE bleak—they have a dark, tragic streak that runs right through them from beginning to end. It has been said that the world is a cruel place for some people some of the time and most people most of the time. Or as the psalmist puts it,

> Our days may come to seventy years,
>   or eighty, if our strength endures;
>   yet the best of them are but trouble and sorrow. (Psalm 90:10)

The Harry Potter character whose life embodies this bleakness more than any other is Severus Snape. Snape is probably the most polarizing character in the whole series—most readers either love him or hate him. I am one of those who love him; in fact, despite his flaws, I confess that Snape is one of my favorite characters in the entire series, the reasons for which will become apparent in this chapter.

Snape's life is comprised of one tragedy after another. We first get a glimpse of this when Snape is giving Harry Occlumency lessons and Harry uses a shield charm, which enables him to see a few brief flashes of Snape's childhood memories: his abusive father, his loneliness, his awkward appearance.[129] Clearly Snape had a rough family life, and things did not get easier for him when he went to Hogwarts. He seems to have been an outcast, and in another memory that Harry witnesses, Snape was the victim of bullying from James and Sirius while the whole school jeered at him. We get the sense that this was not an isolated incident and that Snape was regularly humiliated in front of the whole school by James and Sirius.

This is all complicated by Snape's and Lily Evans's friendship. We learn from Snape's memories at the end of the story that Snape and Lily grew up in neighboring towns and that Snape was the first one to tell Lily that she was a witch. They developed a friendship through this shared bond, which continued on into their time at Hogwarts. Moreover, Snape had a crush on Lily, and his romantic interest in her grew while they were in school together.

At the same time, Snape began dabbling in the Dark Arts, and he surrounded himself with those who were planning on joining Voldemort's Death Eaters. This drove a wedge between him and Lily, and their friendship ultimately came to an end just after the humiliating scene Harry witnessed in the Pensieve, when Snape called Lily a Mudblood. Snape tried to apologize to her later that night, but Lily told him it was the last straw: she could not be the friend of a person who was excited to join the movement that demonized witches with her parentage.[130]

Snape was heartbroken, and he was left to deal with the agony of his unrequited love. This is no small burden. Commenting on Merope Gaunt, Dumbledore says that unrequited love can be so distressing that it saps a person's magical powers.[131] But Snape not only had to deal with Lily's rejection, he also had to watch his bully and archenemy, James Potter, marry the woman he loved—quite a bitter pill to swallow.

After leaving Hogwarts, Snape followed through on his plans to join the Death Eaters, and as a part of his work for Voldemort, he overheard part of the prophecy that Sybill Trelawney made to Dumbledore. When he relayed the prophecy to Voldemort,

Voldemort thought it meant Lily's son, and consequently he decided to murder the whole family. Upon learning this, Snape reached out to Dumbledore to urge him to protect Lily and her family, but to no avail—Voldemort murdered both Lily and James after they made Peter Pettigrew their Secret Keeper at the last second.

Snape was devastated. When Harry sees this scene in the Pensieve, even Snape's face bears the marks of his weeping and misery.[132] His grief is so harrowing that he professes a wish to die; it is a grief that he will carry for the rest of his life. But it does lead to remorse. Snape knows that Lily died to protect her son, and thus Dumbledore makes a request of him: do not let her sacrifice be in vain.[133] This becomes Snape's mission—he pledges to protect Lily's son, but he makes Dumbledore promise to never reveal this because he despised James Potter so much.

This turns out to be much harder than Snape anticipated. Every time he sees Harry, he is reminded of James and the fact that James was the one who married Lily. He takes some of this bitterness out on Harry in Potions classes, and he loses all self-control when Harry watches his father humiliate Snape through the Pensieve. After that incident, he simply cannot stand to be in Harry's presence anymore, and their Occlumency lessons end.

Snape's burdens greaten significantly when Voldemort returns. On the night Voldemort regains his body, Snape returns to him on Dumbledore's orders to pretend to be a double agent for Voldemort. This requires that Snape discern which information he should give Voldemort to persuade him of his loyalty, and which he must keep secret—a difficult and dangerous job indeed given how gifted Voldemort is at Legilimency. It must have been highly demanding and nerve-racking to go back and forth between the two sides, knowing that at any moment his cover could be blown and his life ended. And he carries on like this for three years!

During this time, Dumbledore injures his hand when he puts on Marvolo Gaunt's ring, and Snape tells him that the curse from the ring will begin to spread in about a year. Upon learning this, Dumbledore gives Snape yet another difficult order: Snape must be the one to kill him. He reluctantly agrees to do so, but it is not easy for him to cope with the knowledge that he must kill his friend and mentor, the one who gave him a second chance at life. On at least one occasion he expresses his reservation and takes his anger out on Dumbledore.[134] When the opportunity presents itself, however, Snape does the deed and kills Dumbledore. This is a horrifying prospect in and of itself, but, making matters worse, not a soul knows why he really did it—the Death Eaters celebrate and the Order of the Phoenix vilifies him. Henceforth, he is entirely alone.

Just a year after ending Dumbledore's life, Snape's own life ends. When Voldemort calls him back from the Battle of Hogwarts into the Shrieking Shack and tells him that the Elder Wand is not working properly for him, Snape could have told him the truth. He could have told him that he, Snape, was not the true master of the Elder Wand, which might have saved his life. But he remained silent. And so, Snape's tragic life ends on a tragic note.

When Harry watches these memories one after another in the Pensieve, however, a different picture emerges. Yes, these moments in Snape's life were agonizing and difficult, but it also becomes clear that it is through these tragedies in Snape's life that Voldemort is defeated: Lily's death transforms Snape. The grief drives him to give his life to protect Lily's son—the only hope of defeating Voldemort—even though he is also James Potter's son. Snape's arduous spying on Voldemort supports the work of the Order of the Phoenix. And Snape's murder of Dumbledore wins Voldemort's total trust, enabling him to protect Harry and give him the sword of Gryffindor. It is all part of how the victory is won, of how good triumphs over evil.

The Bible says much the same thing about the suffering of believers. The apostle Paul writes, "Now if we are children, then we are heirs—heirs of God and co-heirs with Christ, if indeed we share in his sufferings in order that we may also share in his glory" (Romans 8:17). The only way to share in the glory and victory of Jesus is through suffering. There is no other path. Paul goes on to describe the anguish of the world as "groaning as in the pains of childbirth," and he says that believers are sharing in this groaning as well (Romans 8:22–23). Moreover, God himself is groaning inside of us as we pray:

> In the same way, the Spirit helps us in our weakness. We do not know what we ought to pray for, but the Spirit himself intercedes for us through wordless groans. And he who searches our hearts knows the mind of the Spirit, because the Spirit intercedes for God's people in accordance with the will of God. (Romans 8:26–27)

Here then is how Jesus' triumph over evil is implemented and how the new world comes to birth: through the pain and suffering of God's people—especially as God's people hold the pain of the world before God in prayer, even when it is too deep to be put into words. Some of this pain, then, is chosen as they linger in prayer with these wordless groans on behalf of others, unsure of what to say but knowing that God is interceding on their behalf as he searches their hearts.[135]

No doubt this is a daunting teaching. None of us want to be told that the only way to victory and glory is through pain. But the insight this teaching brings can also be very comforting—particularly when we are suffering ourselves—because it says that our pain has meaning. That it is part of a larger story. All around us there is chaos and brokenness and groaning. And as Christians, we are right there in the middle of it, feeling the anguish of the world and holding it before God in prayer. But when we look at it through the lens of Romans 8, we find a different story: These groans are actually those of a woman in labor. They are giving way to a new and restored world. And there is no way to the new world except through the birth pains.

This should come as no surprise to Christians because we follow a crucified Messiah who won the victory over evil through suffering. It only follows, then, that we must share in his sufferings in order that we may share in and be a part of implementing that victory. Paul captures it beautifully in another letter:

> But we have this treasure in jars of clay to show that this all-surpassing power is from God and not from us. We are hard pressed on every side, but not crushed;

perplexed, but not in despair; persecuted, but not abandoned; struck down, but not destroyed. We always carry around in our body the death of Jesus, so that the life of Jesus may also be revealed in our body. For we who are alive are always being given over to death for Jesus' sake, so that his life may also be revealed in our mortal body. So then, death is at work in us, but life is at work in you. (2 Corinthians 4:7–12)

The brokenness of these clay jars that are our bodies—the sign of the death of Jesus at work in us—is the means through which the life of Jesus is on display, even if we cannot always see it. Even when we have no idea what to pray. Pain and suffering, then, are not just part of living in a broken world. They are not just forming and shaping our character. They are part of the victory, of how good triumphs over evil.

I have turned to these Bible passages again and again in the personal challenges I have faced. My pain has felt unending and meaningless at times, a bit like Snape's life. And I have known what it is like to pray with groans that cannot be put into words. But when I have stuck my head in the Pensieve—that is, when I have turned to passages like Romans 8 and 2 Corinthians 4—I have found that my prayers and groanings are part of a larger story: They are part of the victory, just as they were for Snape. They are bringing the resurrection life of Jesus into the world. And so "therefore we do not lose heart" (2 Corinthians 4:16).

PART III

The Darkness and the Light

15

Darkness

The trouble is, humans do have a knack of choosing precisely those things that are worst for them.

—ALBUS DUMBLEDORE[136]

HARRY POTTER AND THE *Goblet of Fire* is a turning point in the series. Up until this book, Harry, Ron, and Hermione have certainly faced many challenges: Professor Quirrell trying to steal the Sorcerer's Stone, the opening of the Chamber of Secrets, and the thought-to-be murderer Sirius Black on the loose. But in the fourth book, Lord Voldemort returns. And with his return, the series grows darker and more ominous. Murders become more common, such as those of Bertha Jorkins, Frank Bryce, Mr. Crouch, and Cedric Diggory, and the aura of fear that shrouds the wizarding world becomes more palpable.

This darkness continues to intensify until it reaches a head in the seventh book, by which time an astonishing number of characters have been killed: Sirius Black, Albus Dumbledore, Mad-Eye Moody, Hedwig, Dobby, Fred Weasley, Remus Lupin, Nymphadora Tonks, and Severus Snape, among others. The cruelty and brutality escalate as well (just think of Charity Burbage in Malfoy Manor, the Cattermole family in the Ministry of Magic, or the woman and children who lived in Gregorovitch's old house), and heavier themes are explored (such as Ariana Dumbledore's disturbing ordeal). What is more, the grief and anger that accompany these horrors and deaths are described with poignant detail, so it is hard for readers to miss the growing gloom.

J. K. Rowling was asked about the increasing darkness of the story, particularly since it was intended for children, and her answer was eye-opening:

> I have a real issue with anyone trying to protect children from their own imaginations. And I think that a lot of this goes on. And if we cannot acknowledge and embrace the fact that we all have a certain degree of darkness within us—some more than others, perhaps—and, you know, bring it into the light and examine it and talk about it—this part of the human condition—then I think we will be living in quite a dangerous climate, and I think that's much more damaging for children.[137]

Rowling believes that the human condition entails having a certain degree of darkness inside us—a view quite different from most people shaped by modern, secular culture. The popular view of many people in the United States today is that humans are born essentially good and that it is only the circumstances around us that make us do so-called "evil" things. But as Rowling says, this is not her view, nor is it the way human nature is depicted in Harry Potter. Instead, Harry Potter portrays human nature in line with what Rowling believes—namely, that there is darkness within each of us from the time we are children.

There is a particularly illuminating conversation between Harry and his godfather, Sirius Black, in the Gryffindor common room that bears this all out. In response to Harry saying that Dolores Umbridge is foul enough to be a Death Eater, Sirius responds, "Yes, but the world isn't split into good people and Death Eaters."[138] In other words, the world is not simply divided into good people and bad people. Interestingly, in the movie, he follows that up by saying, "We've all got both light and darkness inside us," which is implied in the first quote and is essentially the same thing Rowling says in her interview.[139]

Another change in the movie is that this conversation takes place just after Harry has the dream where he is Nagini and attacking Mr. Weasley. After the dream, just before he takes a Portkey from Dumbledore's office to go to 12 Grimmauld Place, Dumbledore looks into Harry's eyes and "unbidden, unwanted, but terrifyingly strong, there rose within Harry a hatred so powerful he felt, for that instant, that he would like nothing better than to strike—to bite—to sink his fangs into the man before him."[140] It is as though the snake he had become in the dream is living inside him.

Of course, we later find out that Harry's experience here is due to the connection between him and Voldemort, but it is a vivid image of the way human nature is portrayed in Harry Potter. Humans in Harry Potter are not simply good—it is more complicated than that. They have darkness living inside of them, darkness that not even magic can curb. The Russian novelist Alexander Solzhenitsyn's line about good and evil describes well the world created in Harry Potter: "The line separating good and evil passes not through states, nor between classes, nor between political parties either—but right through every human heart."[141]

While this may not be the view of many people living in the United States today, it is the view presented in the Bible. One of the most well-known characters in the Bible, King David, wrote a couple of poems that illustrate this. In the first, David describes the evil that abounds among the powerful rulers in the world:

> Even from birth the wicked go astray;
>   from the womb they are wayward, spreading lies.
> Their venom is like the venom of a snake,
>   like that of a cobra that has stopped its ears,
> that will not heed the tune of the charmer,
>   however skillful the enchanter may be. (Psalm 58:3–5)

David says that these rulers have been evil from birth. And he describes them as snakes. Their venomous lies have spread throughout the world poisoning people, and their ears have been stopped so they are unable to listen to any who call them out for their actions. As in Harry Potter, "snake" is used here as a symbol of evil, as it is elsewhere in the Bible (see Genesis 3).

But surprisingly, David also admits that *he* has been wicked from birth! The context of this second poem is that David has just committed adultery and murder, and now he has been confronted with it and is admitting it to God. He writes, "Surely I was sinful at birth, sinful from the time my mother conceived me" (Psalm 51:5). It is as if he is saying, "I'm a snake just like these other wicked rulers, and my venom has ruined a lot of people's lives"—his recent murder and adultery being just two obvious examples. King David may be one of the heroes in the Bible, but there is still darkness inside him. Jesus affirms this teaching when he says, "For it is from within, out of a person's heart, that evil thoughts come" (Mark 7:21). And the apostle Paul generalizes this truth to all people when he says, "There is no one righteous, not even one" (Romans 3:10).

The Bible, then, like Harry Potter, teaches that all people have darkness or sin living inside of them that is part of their human condition. But the Bible also teaches that people are not as bad as they could possibly be—there is some "light" inside of them that makes them capable of doing good. This is made possible by what theologians have called God's "common grace." Jesus affirms this idea in the parable he tells about the Good Samaritan (Luke 10:25–37). Samaritans at the time were seen as religious heretics, and Jesus agrees with this characterization (see John 4:22). But he still casts a Samaritan as the hero of his story to demonstrate that all people are capable of moral virtue and of shining some light in the world.

That said, the Bible teaches that the ultimate solution to the darkness inside us is Jesus, the true "light of the world" (John 8:12). As the theologian N. T. Wright puts it,

> Only in the Christian story itself—certainly not in the secular stories of modernity—do we find any sense that the problems of the world are solved not by a straightforward upward movement into the light but by the creator God going down into the dark to rescue humankind and the world from its plight.[142]

God did this chiefly through Jesus' death and resurrection. When Jesus was plunged into darkness on the cross, the darkness inside of us was crucified with him, and we rose with him as "children of the light" (1 Thessalonians 5:5). Because of this, we are transformed into people who share Jesus' identity as "the light of the world," and as such we shine this light into the world through the good that we do (Matthew 5:14–16). And this light shines all the more brilliantly in the midst of evil and darkness—like stars in the night sky (Philippians 2:15). However, there is not just human evil at work in the world; there are darker and more insidious forces of evil at work, which is something we find in Harry Potter as well.

One of the revelations in the seventh book is that Dumbledore had a friendship with Gellert Grindelwald when they were teenagers. And as this relationship is divulged, we begin to learn just how evil Grindelwald was. In fact, there are clear overtones that his rise to power is being compared with the Nazi regime: he is a blond-haired, blue-eyed wizard from central Europe who is defeated by a British wizard (Dumbledore) in 1945; he was expelled from Durmstrang for his "experiments"; and the castle where he imprisoned his enemies (which was where he was imprisoned after he was defeated) was called Nurmengard (note that the Nazi war criminals were tried in Nuremberg, Germany). Grindelwald believed in a magical ruling class in which Muggles were to be subjugated, and he was willing to do whatever it took to achieve what he thought to be "the greater good."

Though Dumbledore eventually confronts and defeats him, Grindelwald's ideas do not die. They simply morph, and just a few decades later they become the foundation of a new regime: Voldemort's. In other words, evil simply takes on a new form. After Dumbledore dies, Harry reflects on how Dumbledore told him this during his first year at Hogwarts after his first encounter with Voldemort. Dumbledore said that the battle against evil was, in a sense, a losing battle, but it was still important to keep fighting it, "for only then could evil be kept at bay, though never quite eradicated."[143] If you hold evil at bay, it will simply pop up in a new way. Or as Snape says, the Dark Arts are like a many-headed monster such that if you cut off one head, a more powerful one will sprout in its place.[144] This evil goes beyond simply human evil and shows up again and again over generations. Just like the darkness in Voldemort's cave, it is "somehow denser than normal darkness."[145]

The Bible's teaching on the evil in our world is similar. The apostle Paul writes, "Put on the full armor of God, so that you can take your stand against the devil's schemes. For our struggle is not against flesh and blood, but against the rulers, against the authorities, against the powers of this dark world and against the spiritual forces of evil in the heavenly realms" (Ephesians 6:11–12). Standing behind the human evil we face are dark, supernatural forces. The book of Revelation teaches that these dark forces stood behind the tyrannical regime of the Roman Empire, and by extension all the tyrannical regimes that came before and after—Nazi Germany being just one obvious example (Revelation 13). These powers simply morph over time through the manifold oppressive empires that have reigned throughout history, and each regime is simply the latest manifestation of these dark spiritual forces that have partnered with human evil, much like the regimes of Grindelwald and Voldemort.

Given that there is darkness in our world, how should we respond to it? It might be tempting to turn to violence and military power. Sirius Black points out that this was how Barty Crouch dealt with Voldemort's supporters: "Crouch fought violence with violence, and authorized the use of the Unforgiveable Curses against suspects."[146] Similarly, Cornelius Fudge tried to use the power of dark creatures—dementors—to bring stability and peace to the wizarding world. But Dumbledore's strategy was to fight hate with love: "Lord Voldemort's gift for spreading discord and enmity is very great. We can fight it only by showing an equally strong bond of friendship and trust."[147]

Indeed, this is also how Jesus calls his followers to respond to evil. He modeled this when he prayed for his killers while hanging from the cross: "Father, forgive them, for they do not know what they are doing" (Luke 23:34). Christians are called to follow his example:

Do not take revenge, my dear friends, but leave room for God's wrath, for it is written: "It is mine to avenge; I will repay," says the Lord. On the contrary: "If your enemy is hungry, feed him; if he is thirsty, give him something to drink. In doing this, you will heap burning coals on his head." Do not be overcome by evil, but overcome evil with good. (Romans 12:19–21)

Only good can overcome evil, for if evil is used to overcome evil, evil wins. Or as Martin Luther King Jr. famously said, "Darkness cannot drive out darkness: only light can do that. Hate cannot drive out hate: only love can do that."[148]

16

Courage

Only a true Gryffindor could have pulled that *out of the hat,*
Harry.

—ALBUS DUMBLEDORE[149]

IF LOVE IS THE most important virtue in the Harry Potter series,
courage is not far behind. Indeed, Hermione highlights the importance of both when she encourages Harry as he is about to go
through the final door that will lead him to Quirrell (and Voldemort). Hermione tells Harry that he is a great wizard, to which
he responds that he is not as good as her. But then she says, "Me!
Books and cleverness! There are more important things—friendship and bravery and—oh Harry, be *careful!*"[150] Friendship and
bravery. Love and courage. In Harry Potter, these are the chief
traits that distinguish a person of great character.

Dumbledore gives an apt description of courage in his speech
to the school just after Voldemort returns: "Remember, if the time
should come when you have to make a choice between what is
right and what is easy, remember what happened to a boy who
was good, and kind, and brave, because he strayed across the path
of Lord Voldemort. Remember Cedric Diggory."[151] Courage is
choosing to do what is right over what is easy when the two are
in conflict. It is resisting evil even when it is costly. This is why

Dumbledore says, in reference to Harry asking the Sorting Hat to place him in Gryffindor over Slytherin, "It is our choices, Harry, that show what we truly are, far more than our abilities."[152]

The most admirable characters in Harry Potter understand this. Certainly the members of the Order of the Phoenix do, who fight Voldemort and his followers despite being severely outnumbered and not having the support of the Ministry of Magic. Sirius Black captures their spirit well when he says to the Weasley twins, after their father has been bitten by Nagini, "There are things worth dying for!"[153] Doing good and resisting evil are worth it no matter what the costs. And of course, Sirius practices what he preaches when he makes the ultimate sacrifice while protecting Harry and his friends from Death Eaters in the Department of Mysteries.

On the other hand, Cornelius Fudge and the Ministry of Magic succumb to fear when Voldemort returns. As Sirius shrewdly observes of Fudge, "It's so much more comfortable to convince himself Dumbledore's lying to destabilize him."[154] Fudge knows that if Voldemort is really back, it means major sacrifices will have to be made, and he does not want to face this possibility. So he chooses what is easy over what is right.

But courage is not just required when facing our enemies— we need courage as well when we are confronting friends. Dumbledore says as much at the end of the first book when he is awarding the final points for the House Cup: "It takes a great deal of bravery to stand up to our enemies, but just as much to stand up to our friends."[155] Neville, unsure if he really belongs in Gryffindor, had confronted Harry, Ron, and Hermione about leaving the common room at night, and consequently Dumbledore awarded him ten points for his courage. Luna Lovegood is similarly admired by Harry for her knack for speaking uncomfortable truths. Anyone who has had to confront a friend knows just how much courage it takes to do this.

The summary of virtue in Harry Potter is choosing to do what is right even when, or rather especially when, it is difficult and costly—a sentiment that is quite different from that of American consumeristic culture, which encourages people to do and buy whatever makes them happy and comfortable. It is countercultural virtue. And undergirding this virtue is courage; as Maya Angelou said, "Courage is the most important of all the virtues, because without courage you can't practice any other virtue consistently. You can practice any virtue erratically, but nothing consistently without courage."[156] It takes courage to practice all the other virtues when it hurts us to do so.

If it takes courage to do what is right, it also takes love to be courageous. There is a deep union between the two chief virtues in Harry Potter, and the character who exemplifies this more than any other is Severus Snape. As chapter 14 demonstrated, Snape faced many trials throughout his life that required great courage of him. Dumbledore is so impressed by this that he even wonders aloud to Snape, "I sometimes think we Sort too soon," implying that Snape's bravery is a trait more commonly found among Gryffindors than Slytherins.[157]

But at the very end of the series, when Harry watches Snape's memories, we learn what sustained Snape's courage all along. After Lily dies and Snape is weeping in Dumbledore's office, Dumbledore suggests a way forward for him: if he really loved Lily Evans, he should make sure that she did not die in vain.[158] In other words, the request Dumbledore makes of Snape—that he help Dumbledore protect Lily's son—is rooted in Snape's love for Lily.

And that love endured for the rest of his life. Dumbledore eventually tells Snape that Harry must die in order to defeat Voldemort, and Snape is outraged. He feels betrayed and used because he thought all his spying and duplicity were for the purpose of keeping Lily's son alive. And now, it seems, Dumbledore is pulling a bait and switch. Dumbledore is surprised that Snape reacts so strongly to hearing that Harry must die, and he asks Snape if he has begun to truly care for Harry. Snape shouts, "For *him*?"[159] And he casts the Patronus charm, causing the silver doe to appear and prance around the office before soaring out the window. Dumbledore is moved to tears as he recognizes the doe to be Lily's Patronus—evidence that Snape still loves Lily. Amazed, Dumbledore asks Snape if his love has really persisted all these years—to which Snape gives his famous response: "Always."[160]

Snape's love for Lily was the source of his courage. It is what braced him to endure the grueling ordeal—even unto death—that was demanded of him in his work for Dumbledore to protect Lily's son. And Harry honors that courage by naming his son Albus *Severus*. To calm his son's fears about the possibility of being sorted into Slytherin House, Harry tells him that he was named after two former Hogwarts Headmasters: "One of them was a Slytherin and he was probably the bravest man I ever knew."[161]

The courage-creating power of love is attested to in the Bible as well. First Corinthians 13, the apostle Paul's famous chapter on love, says, "Love always hopes, always perseveres" (13:7). There is a sustaining nature to true love that makes people press on no matter what it costs for the sake of their beloved. And in no one is this clearer than Jesus himself.

As a popular but also notorious prophet, Jesus faced many tests to his courage throughout his ministry, but the most significant one happened just before he was crucified. Jesus knew his death was near, and understandably it was deeply distressing to him. So he prayed and asked God to spare him what lay ahead. But his request was denied him; the only way for the mission to be completed was for Jesus to go to the cross (Matthew 26:36–46). So he stayed the course—he chose to do what was right even though it cost him his life.

When one early Christian writer described Jesus' motivation for doing this, they said, "For the joy set before him he endured the cross, scorning its shame, and sat down at the right hand of the throne of God" (Hebrews 12:2). Jesus endured the cross because of the joy on the other side, the joy of having done his Father's will and all the good that would come from it. Or as the poet and writer Jackie Hill Perry puts it: "Jesus didn't endure because He was strong; He was most likely at one of the weakest points of His humanity, but He endured because He loved His God. Therefore, He was fully committed to doing the will of God, no matter the cost."[162] It was *love* that gave Jesus the courage to face the cross. Love for God. Love for humanity. And love for all of creation.

Jesus' example is the model for us as we strive for courage. We are in desperate need of courage today; there are manifold injustices that, like Goliaths, reign in terror because they go un-challenged: violence, war, human trafficking, poverty, disease, rac-ism, corruption, and the destruction of creation, among others. So many are like the armies of Israel shaking in their boots on the hillside opting for what is easy over what is right (1 Samuel 17). When we are afraid and tempted to join their ranks, what often inspires us is an exemplar of courage, a champion. King David was this champion for the Israelites, and this is why Dumbledore tells the Hogwarts students to remember *their* champion, Cedric Dig-gory, when he exhorts them to choose what is right over what is easy—remembering what Cedric endured will inspire the students to persevere in the difficult days ahead.

For Christians, Jesus Christ is our exemplar, our champion. This is why the writer of the Letter to the Hebrews says to "[fix] our eyes on Jesus, the pioneer and perfecter of faith" and to "con-sider him who endured such opposition from sinners, so that you will not grow weary and lose heart" (Hebrews 12:2–3). The path to courage is found in Jesus. For those who are weary in doing good and tempted to quit because it would be more comfortable, remember how Jesus resisted the powers that stood against him— the chief priests and Herod and Pontius Pilate and demons and Satan himself—even to the point of death on a cross. Remember that he did so because of his great love for you. And when we re-member this, we find that "the Messiah's love makes us press on" (2 Corinthians 5:14 NTfE). In other words, when you are forced to choose between what is right and what is easy, remember Jesus and what choosing to do the right thing cost him, and it will spark your courage.

17

Suffering

And quite honestly . . . I've had enough trouble for a lifetime.

—HARRY POTTER[163]

ONE OF THE THEMES that I hope has come through in this book is that Harry Potter is very stark in its portrayal of pain and suffering. This is partly what makes the story so relatable for many people. We have all tasted sorrow in this world to one degree or another, so to have a story speak so realistically about it—even though it is fiction—is very fitting and rings true. This is also in part why the story has been so impactful to me. When I started to deal with health issues a few years ago and was learning to cope with them, I found that the Harry Potter series could speak movingly to my pain—not because it told me how I should deal with it; rather, it filled my imagination with a vision in which suffering could be meaningful and could change me for the better—a message that we also find in the Bible and which is so hard to find anywhere else in our culture today.

Paul Brand, a doctor who started his career in India and then moved to the United States, made the following observation: "In the United States . . . I encountered a society that seeks to avoid pain at all costs. Patients lived at a greater comfort level than any I had previously treated, but they seemed far less equipped to handle suffering and far more traumatized by it."[164] It begs the question: why does our modern, secular society struggle so much (comparatively) with handling suffering? Much could be said here, but the philosopher John Gray, who is not himself religious, makes an insightful point:

> Religious cultures could admit that earthly life was hard, for they promised another in which all tears would be wiped away. Their humanist successors affirm something still more incredible—that in the future, even the near future, everyone can be happy. Societies founded on a faith in progress cannot admit the normal unhappiness of human life.[165]

If there is no meaning to be found beyond this life, it is very difficult to conceive of how suffering can actually benefit a person. And this often leads to ignorance of the brokenness in our world when suffering is far from us (or we choose not to see it) and deep despair when it comes near. This is, of course, not to say that suffering is necessarily going to change a person for the better. Jonathan Haidt, a psychologist, has noted that people who walk through particularly distressing hardships often develop post-traumatic stress disorder which can make them "anxious and over reactive" and more likely to "panic or crumble more easily when faced with later adversity."[166]

That said, Haidt also found that some people who go through these very same stressful situations experience "post-traumatic growth." They are far more resilient than they were before, and they have a greater capacity for "sympathy, love, and forgiveness" that leads to deeper relationships. They also rethink what is most important to them and are more likely to devote themselves to principles larger than themselves, such as God or some kind of spirituality.[167]

This is why the message of Harry Potter is so helpful for the time and place in which we live. It is realistic about the trauma that suffering can cause, but it also says that it is possible for suffering to change a person for the better. And it explores what this looks like, especially in the character of Harry himself.

There are two important conversations between Dumbledore and Harry that bear this all out. The first one happens in Dumbledore's office at the end of the fifth book just after Sirius has died. In this scene, Harry's grief is very raw, and he is also irate and lashing out at Dumbledore because he does not want to talk about what just happened. But in response, Dumbledore tells Harry that it is not wrong to feel such strong emotions, and moreover, "the fact that you can feel pain like this is your greatest strength."[168]

Later in their conversation, Dumbledore says this quality of Harry's is why Voldemort was unable to possess him in the Ministry of Magic earlier that night. When he attempted to, and Harry felt that the agony of it would kill him, he begins to think, "*I'll see Sirius again. . . .* And as Harry's heart filled with emotion, the creature's coils loosened, the pain was gone."[169] Something similar happens after Dobby dies in the seventh book. While Harry was in Malfoy Manor, Voldemort's thoughts kept infiltrating his mind, diverting his attention from the severity of his predicament. But when he began digging Dobby's grave and mourning his loss, Voldemort's thoughts could not penetrate his mind. His grief functioned like a shield.[170] According to Dumbledore, this capacity to feel grief and love is what the prophecy meant when it said, "But he will have power the Dark Lord knows not," and he unpacks this more in a second conversation he has with Harry at the end of the sixth book.[171]

This conversation also takes place in Dumbledore's office, where Dumbledore and Harry are discussing how to finish Voldemort in light of learning about his Horcruxes. Dumbledore reiterates that Harry's rare skill and power that will give him a chance against Voldemort is his ability to love, but this time he goes into more detail about how Harry got that power. On one level, Dumbledore says that, given how much Harry has suffered, the fact that he can love at all is remarkable.[172] As Jonathan Haidt observed, many people are hardened by their pain and become less capable of love.

But the suffering Harry has had to endure throughout his short life has neither embittered him towards the world nor caused him to crumble easily; it has formed in him the capacity to love. And much of this is because he knows what it is like to be on the receiving end of the abuse of power. He endured constant bullying from his cousin Dudley and his gang, as well as harsh and cruel parenting—all of it during the most formative years of his life. This produced empathy in him towards those who have experienced similar ill treatment, even towards a sworn enemy: after watching his father bully Snape in a memory, Harry finds himself feeling sorry for him because he had been in Snape's shoes before and knew how horrible it was to be publicly humiliated.[173]

When he turns eleven, though, Harry learns that the reason he had to suffer at the hand of the Dursleys in the first place was that Voldemort killed his parents. And Voldemort would be the source of all of Harry's future suffering—both in Voldemort's repeated attempts to kill him and by sending his Death Eaters to murder the people whom Harry loved. This is why Dumbledore says it is *Voldemort* who made Harry who he is.

It was Voldemort's initial attack on baby Harry that imparted to him the ability to look into Voldemort's mind and speak Parseltongue. Yet, despite sharing some of Voldemort's powers— the dream of any Death Eater—Harry never once wanted to join Voldemort for the obvious reason that Voldemort was the one who killed Harry's parents.[174] More remarkably, Harry also never wanted to depose of Voldemort through using the Dark Arts against him. Because Harry knows what it is like to be oppressed, he has no desire to join the oppressor or be the oppressor. The love and empathy that were formed in him through his childhood sufferings have protected him from wanting power for himself.

This is why Dumbledore says to Harry at the very end of the story, "You are the worthy possessor of the Hallows."[175] I cannot help but think that Harry's selflessness, loyalty, sympathy, innocence, and *love* stem from the fact that he has suffered so much for someone his age. As Horace Slughorn says regarding love potions, "It is impossible to manufacture or imitate love"—but it is often forged in the fire of suffering.[176] Or as Chaim Potok put it in his novel *The Chosen*,

"One learns of the pain of others by suffering one's own pain. . . . In the silence . . . he [begins] to hear the world crying."[177]

It is worth noting that something very similar happens to Dumbledore himself. Like Harry, Dumbledore lost his parents at a fairly young age, and he also lost his sister, which was complicated by the fact that he played a role in her death and thus felt life-long guilt for it. This also broke the friendship he had with Gellert Grindelwald and estranged him from his brother. Elphias Doge, Dumbledore's friend, recounts the effect these losses had on the young Dumbledore in his obituary. After traveling the world for a year upon graduation from Hogwarts—during which time these tragedies happened—Doge returned to find that Dumbledore had changed substantially: he was more sympathetic and caring, though less jovial.[178]

Putting it all together, what we find in Harry Potter is that loss, grief, and suffering have the potential to grow a person's character and make them more loving, compassionate, and resilient. The Bible teaches this as well. It does so in a number of ways, but one of them is through the metaphor of discipline. In the Letter to the Hebrews, suffering is compared to both a father's discipline of his children and an athlete's discipline in preparing for a race. Building on this analogy, the writer says, "No discipline seems pleasant at the time, but painful. Later on, however, it produces a harvest of righteousness and peace for those who have been trained by it" (Hebrews 12:11). Suffering might be painful for the moment, but if we persevere through it, like discipline, it will transform us for the better. It will yield the fruit of righteousness and peace in our lives. We will become more kind and patient people to be around.

Another metaphor the Bible uses for suffering is fire. The apostle Peter says it like this:

> In [your coming salvation] you greatly rejoice, though now for a little while you may have had to suffer grief in all kinds of trials. These have come so that the proven genuineness of your faith—of greater worth than gold, which perishes even though refined by fire—may result

in praise, glory, and honor when Jesus Christ is revealed.
(1 Peter 1:6–7)

Just as fire purifies gold by burning away its impurities, so suffering refines our character by "burning" away our flaws. Courage is formed because, after surviving a particular hardship, a person is more confident that future challenges can be overcome; therefore, they are more likely to choose to do what is right even when it is costly. And love is formed because a person who knows what it is like to face adversity is more likely to extend grace and patience to others who are having a difficult time.

The natural question to ask in light of all this is: Why do some people change for the better when they undergo suffering and others do not? For instance, why do Harry and Dumbledore come out on the other side of the pain they experienced in their adolescent years as more compassionate and courageous people, while Voldemort is hardened and embittered by his own childhood suffering? That is a very complex question that we could never answer fully, but I will make one observation: When Harry and Dumbledore suffered, they let themselves feel the pain of their losses. They grieved. They adopted a posture of vulnerability and submission. Voldemort, on the other hand, chose the path of secrecy and independence and detested the very idea of feeling pain because it was a sign of weakness.

The Bible, again, teaches the very same thing. There are a number of ways that the Bible calls us to respond to pain and suffering, but one is especially fitting here. In Tim Keller's excellent book *Walking with God through Pain and Suffering*, he shows that the Bible often describes suffering through the metaphor of walking through fire (or through darkness or flood). But in calling us to *walk* through the "furnace," the Bible "keeps us from thinking we can run from the furnace (avoid it) or quickly run through it (deny it) or just lie down hopelessly (despair in it)."[179] This is what Harry and Dumbledore do. They *walk* through the fire. They grieve their losses. They submit. And it changes them for the better.

A number of chapters in this book have discussed pain and suffering, and each one has approached it from a different angle, but they have all converged on one person: Jesus of Nazareth. He is at the heart of it all, for "in him all things hold together" (Colossians 1:17). And likewise, when we think about suffering as a fire that we must walk through, and which has the power to transform us for the better, we must end with Jesus, the one who said to his followers, "And surely, I am with you always, to the very end of the age" (Matthew 28:20). Or as the ancient prophecy said,

> When you pass through the waters,
>   I will be with you;
> and when you pass through the rivers,
>   they will not sweep over you.
> When you walk through the fire,
>   you will not be burned;
>   the flames will not set you ablaze. (Isaiah 43:2)

18

Death

And he knew, without knowing how he knew it, that the phoenix had gone, had left Hogwarts for good, just as Dumbledore had left the school, had left the world . . . had left Harry.[180]

J. K. ROWLING ONCE said in an interview, "I think about death and dying every single day of my life"—so it should come as no surprise that death is a major theme in the Harry Potter books.[181] In fact, Rowling has said that the entire series can be encapsulated in a couple of lines from the last book, one of which deals with death.[182] It is engraved on the tombstone of Harry's parents in the graveyard in Godric's Hollow, and it reads: "*The last enemy that shall be destroyed is death.*"[183] This line is the second of two explicit references from the Bible that appear in the Harry Potter series, and it comes from 1 Corinthians 15:26 in a letter that the apostle Paul wrote to a church. It is part of a larger chapter dealing with the resurrection of Jesus, but the point that Rowling seems to be drawing from it is that death is the last and greatest enemy of humanity.

This comes out especially in "The Tale of the Three Brothers." In the tale, three brothers encounter Death, a hooded figure, as they cross a bridge that they magically conjured to avoid a treacherous river. Death is personified here as a cunning and larger-than-life figure, and even though Dumbledore says that he thinks it is a legend that Death created the Deathly Hallows for the three brothers, he still refers to "Death" (with a capital D) at one point in a later conversation with Harry (more on that to come).[184] So Death may not be a literal person in Harry Potter, but it is in some sense a crafty enemy.

I am not sure how many people in the United States today think of death as a great enemy. Perhaps if they have just lost a loved one and are grieving, then they are likely to be well-aware of the ravages of death, but we are more often told to think of death as a natural part of life and to simply accept it. Of course, death is natural in that everyone dies, but for many people it is very difficult to accept and seems very *un*natural. Just like the refrain in Edgar Allan Poe's poem "The Raven," we feel the sting and despair of "Nevermore."[185] Death is irreversible, and along with it go our friends and family, our bodies and health, our work and hobbies, our passions and dreams—everything in our lives that we hold dear, never to be had again.

This often evokes fear in us. In his Pulitzer Prize-winning book *The Denial of Death*, Ernest Becker argues that whether or not we experience a fear of death, it motivates everything we do: "The idea of death, the fear of it, haunts the human animal like nothing else; it is a mainspring of human activity—activity designed largely to avoid the fatality of death, to overcome it by denying in some way that it is the final destiny for man."[186] Put another way, according to Becker, death is an enemy we all fear subconsciously if not consciously.

And of course, given that Rowling is quoting a verse from a very important chapter in the Bible, the notion that death is an enemy is a pervasive theme here as well. In the passage that Rowling quotes on the Potters' tombstone, the apostle Paul is saying that death is an enemy that will at last be defeated when God raises his people from the dead just as he raised Jesus (1 Corinthians 15:20–28). The Bible also teaches that humanity is "held in slavery by their fear of death" (Hebrews 2:15). And like "The Tale of the Three Brothers," Death is personified in the Bible, but this time as a rider on a pale horse who kills "by sword, famine and plague, and by the wild beasts of the earth" (Revelation 6:8). So according to the Bible, Death is an enemy who ravages the world, and there will be no hope until this enemy is defeated.

But how is death to be defeated? This question is at the very heart of the plot in Harry Potter. Voldemort's highest goal is to conquer death, and thus he aptly calls his followers Death Eaters. He sheds some light on his strategy to defeat death when he recounts to his Death Eaters how he survived after his failed attempt to kill baby Harry: "I, who have gone further than anybody along the path that leads to immortality. You know my goal—to conquer death. And now . . . it appeared that one or more of my experiments had worked."[187] It is later revealed that these "experiments" are his Horcruxes—objects that he has hidden part of his soul in. These protected his soul from his own rebounded curse, which should have killed him. Dumbledore believes that Voldemort is the only wizard in history to ever make more than one Horcrux, and therefore Dumbledore says that Voldemort is "immortal . . . or as close to immortal as any man can be."[188]

Dumbledore also sheds light on why Voldemort chose to use Horcruxes in his pursuit of immortality as opposed to acquiring a Sorcerer's Stone. Even though the Elixir of Life (which is produced from a Sorcerer's Stone) could make one immortal, Dumbledore says that Voldemort would have detested the idea of being dependent on drinking the Elixir regularly into eternity to stave off death. There were too many possibilities for something to go wrong.[189]

Thus, fundamentally, Voldemort is after *independence* in his quest for immortality. He thinks that death is a "shameful human weakness," and he is willing to do whatever he can to free himself from it.[190] As it turns out, both Harry and Dumbledore also chase immortality for brief periods of their lives—except they do it in their quest for the Deathly Hallows. And in both cases, their quest makes them blind to reality and callous towards those they love.

In Dumbledore's case, it happens when Gellert Grindelwald shows up in Godric's Hollow the summer after Dumbledore graduates from Hogwarts. The two of them make their plans to search for the Deathly Hallows—to become the masters of death—but their obsession with the Hallows causes Dumbledore to forget the responsibility he has to care for his frail sister. Aberforth confronts him about this, and the situation spirals out of control. Dumbledore's quest for immortality and invincibility warped his conception of reality, and it ended up costing his sister's life.[191]

Harry, likewise, upon learning about the Deathly Hallows, becomes consumed with finding them. And it causes him to ignore his mission of destroying Horcruxes and to become indifferent towards his friends. One night in particular he fixates on the Hallows to the point of forgetting that Luna is locked in Azkaban (so he believed). But merely thinking of the dementors guarding Azkaban draws his mind back to the invincibility of the Elder Wand and to obsession over the Hallows.[192]

Just like Voldemort, then, both Dumbledore and Harry seek immortality for the sake of invincibility. And it changes them for the worse. This approach to conquering death is an ancient one, according to the Bible. In fact, it is at the very heart of humanity's rebellion against God. At the beginning of the Bible's story, in the garden of Eden, Adam and Eve were free to eat from any tree they desired except one—the tree in the middle of the garden. They were told by God that if they ate of that tree they would die. Then one day a serpent, the embodiment of evil, comes along and tells Eve that if she eats of the prohibited tree, "You will not certainly die. . . . For God knows that when you eat from it your eyes will be opened, and you will be like God, knowing good and evil" (Genesis 3:4–5). The passage goes on: "When the woman saw that the fruit of the tree was good for food and pleasing to the eye, and also desirable for gaining wisdom, she took some and ate it" (Genesis 3:6).

The offer the serpent makes is enticing: "You will be like God. You will be independent. You will not need him or anyone else." And Eve buys it: she recognizes that the fruit is "desirable for gaining wisdom"—the wisdom of God, according to the serpent—and thus she eats from the tree. This is the approach Voldemort takes to conquering death. He is in pursuit of independence, invincibility, immortality. In short, he wants to be godlike. But as in the case of Adam and Eve, it leads to his ruin.

There is another path to conquering death that we see in Harry Potter, though, and this is the approach that Harry ultimately takes. There is a crucial moment in the seventh book when Harry knows that Voldemort is about to get the Elder Wand, and he has to choose who to question first: Griphook or Ollivander. Griphook can tell him about Gringotts vaults and the potential of finding another Horcrux, while Ollivander can tell him about the Elder Wand. And Harry chooses Horcruxes over Hallows. He talks to Griphook first, and Voldemort ends up with the Elder Wand. Forgoing the chance to get the unbeatable wand might seem foolish, as Ron's incredulous reaction indicates, but it is a sign of Harry's renewed trust in Dumbledore's wisdom.[193] He embraces weakness, not knowing where it will lead him.

But eventually, after seeing Snape's memories in the Pensieve, Harry realizes that this path must end with his death in order for Voldemort to be beatable. So he walks into the Forbidden Forest, and Voldemort hits him with a Killing Curse. To Harry's surprise though, he winds up in King's Cross Station, and he meets Dumbledore there, who tells him that Harry is not dead. Harry is surprised by this because he knows full well that he had just been hit with a Killing Curse. But Dumbledore sums it all up at the end of their conversation when he tells Harry, "You are the true master of death, because the true master does not seek to run away from Death."[194]

Ultimately, then, the way that Harry conquers death is through dying. The last and greatest enemy is defeated by surrendering to it. The inscription on the tombstone that sits over the Potters' rotting bodies about awaiting the defeat of death is fulfilled in their son's death. It is a shocking turn of events; but it is also the story we find in the Bible.

The Bible teaches that Jesus Christ is the true master of death, the one who "holds the keys of death" (Revelation 1:18). And just like Harry, the way he conquered death was by dying, by submitting to death: "Since the children have flesh and blood, he too shared in their humanity so that by his death he might break the power of him who holds the power of death—that is, the devil" (Hebrews 2:14).

In another wonderful passage, the apostle Paul explains how this happens:

> When the perishable has been clothed with the imperishable, and the mortal with immortality, then the saying that is written will come true: "Death has been swallowed up in victory."
>
> "Where, O death, is your victory?
> Where, O death, is your sting?"
>
> The sting of death is sin, and the power of sin is the law. But thanks be to God! He gives us the victory through our Lord Jesus Christ. (1 Corinthians 15:54–57)

When he says that the sting of death is sin, we might say that death is being likened to a bee whose stinger is sin—if you get stung with the poison of sin, you will die. But by dying, Jesus took the poison upon himself—he dealt with sin and thus broke the stinger. And when he did that, death lost its power. The bee became harmless. Death was defeated. And the evidence of this was that Jesus was raised from the dead. As the apostle Peter says, "God raised [Jesus] from the dead, freeing him from the agony of death, because it was impossible for death to keep its hold on him" (Acts 2:24).

Because Jesus conquered death through his death, there is hope for humanity. He has reversed the destruction that Adam brought into the world through his sin: "For as in Adam all die, so in Christ all will be made alive" (1 Corinthians 15:22). Though death still ravages our world, Jesus' resurrection is evidence of death's final demise, just as the "firstfruits" of a crop give evidence that the rest of the harvest will come (1 Corinthians 15:20–28). "The covering that is cast over all peoples, the veil that is spread over all nations"—like the veil that Sirius fell through in the Department of Mysteries—will one day be finally destroyed (Isaiah 25:7–8 ESV).

This is the biblical basis for hope. Yes, we still grieve when our loved ones die, but for those who believe in Jesus, we can grieve with hope. We can look death in the eyes without fear, recognize it for the enemy it is without having to justify it as "natural," and know that it has been defeated. Or as the poet George Herbert said of death,

> For where thou only wert before
> An executioner at best;
> Thou art a gard'ner now.[195]

Death is still the enemy, but instead of merely burying our bodies in graveyards, he is forced to plant us as seeds—and one day we will shoot up through the ground. The tombs will break open. The last enemy shall be defeated. And "death shall be no more" (Revelation 21:4 ESV).

19

The Cave

I've been better. . . . That potion . . . was no health drink. . . .

—ALBUS DUMBLEDORE[196]

AS I HAVE BEEN writing this book and reflecting on the Harry Potter series, there are two characters who come up again and again: Dumbledore and Harry. There are many heroes in Harry Potter, but these two rise to the top. No one does more or sacrifices more to bring down Voldemort, and these last two chapters will be an ode to them. In particular, these chapters will unpack the moment that each of them is plunged into darkness in order that the light might overcome it, beginning with Dumbledore.

Dumbledore's character plays a few different biblical roles in the Harry Potter series. We have already seen how he plays a God-the-Father-like role in chapter 9 as he serves as the mastermind of the plan that Harry, like Jesus, must trust and follow. J. K. Rowling has also referred to Dumbledore as John the Baptist to Harry's Christ as he prepares the way for Harry but in some ways is inferior to him, as Dumbledore acknowledges in their reunion at King's Cross Station.[197] But Dumbledore also plays a Christ role, and this happens chiefly in the scene where he and Harry go to Voldemort's cave to destroy one of his Horcruxes.

Dumbledore begins to embody this Christ role before they even get inside the cave when he cuts his forearm with a knife to make a blood payment to open a way in.[198] This notion of a blood payment is a very rich idea in the Bible, as Jesus' blood is referred to as the precious payment that was made to redeem humans from their "empty way of life" (1 Peter 1:18–19).

Upon entering the cave, Harry and Dumbledore find that they are on the shore of a large, black lake with an island in the middle of it. The island is emitting a greenish glow, and once they get there, they find that it is coming from a basin full of an emerald potion. Because the Horcrux is in the potion (or so they think), Dumbledore thinks of all the possible ways that the potion can be removed, and he eventually concludes that the only way to get rid of it is to drink it. He conjures a crystal goblet and tells Harry, despite his objections, that Harry must force him to keep drinking the liquid no matter how badly Dumbledore wants him to stop. He is thus very aware that the potion is likely to harm him in some way.

And harm him it does. He drinks three gobletfuls of the potion, but while he is drinking the fourth, he falls into the side of the basin and begins to have a hallucination. He closes his eyes as if he were having a nightmare, and he cries again and again that he does not want to drink any more of the potion. He no longer has the strength to hold the goblet steady, and at this point, Harry takes over filling up the goblet and forcing Dumbledore to drink it.[199]

After the fifth gobletful, Dumbledore begins to scream. After the sixth, he falls to his knees and begins to shake uncontrollably. He sobs with tremendous guilt acknowledging some past wrongdoing and promising to never do it again.[200] After the seventh, he continues to yell and scream, and he moans his desire to be hurt in place of an unnamed "them."[201] The agony continues to grow. After the tenth gobletful, Dumbledore shrieks in torment, "Make it stop, make it stop, I want to die!"[202] After the eleventh, he shouts, "KILL ME!"[203] And after the twelfth, he gasps, rolls over onto his face, and becomes unconscious.

Dumbledore is not the only character who drinks the pernicious potion; both Kreacher and Regulus Black drank it, and both suffered its horrors. One effect of the potion is that it causes such extreme thirst that the drinker is forced to scoop water from the lake and consequently awaken the army of Inferi lying below the surface. But the other effect is that the drinker is forced to relive their worst memories—much like they would when in the suffocating power of a dementor's presence, only in this case there is no Patronus that one can summon to one's defense. The weight of the memories must be borne, and it takes a severe toll on the one who must bear it.

We never see Dumbledore like this at any other point in the story. Dumbledore is mostly a kindhearted and peaceful old man who enjoys good humor. Sometimes he appears to be very burdened, and occasionally he erupts in fury, particularly when his students are threatened. But he never unravels like he does in the cave. This is shocking behavior for a man who at every other moment in the series is quite composed.

But such is the effect of the potion. Through Dumbledore's sobs and screams, we do get hints as to what he is experiencing. He talks about something being his fault, so clearly he has a lot of guilt. And he also says that he does not want "them" to be hurt. But at the end of the seventh book, we find out why Dumbledore was in such agony. It happens just after Aberforth, Dumbledore's brother, saves Harry, Ron, and Hermione when they Apparate into Hogsmeade. Aberforth begins to cast doubt on his brother's motives and questions if he really cared for others, and it all comes to a head when Aberforth says that Albus was finally free when Ariana died. Harry protests and discloses, having connected the dots, why it was torture for Dumbledore to drink the potion: "He thought he was watching Grindelwald hurting you and Ariana."[204]

Dumbledore was never free; he was burdened with the guilt of precipitating his sister's death for the rest of his life. And he was being forced to relive it in full when he drank the potion. Dumbledore confirms this in King's Cross Station when he discloses to Harry his crushing fear that he might have been the one who cast the curse that took Ariana's life.[205] One would hardly expect drinking a potion to cause such agony—more agony, it would seem, than any physical pain Voldemort could have inflicted on his trespassers. But so it is.

And in drinking the emerald potion, Dumbledore echoes Jesus. "Cup" is a rich image in the Bible, but one of its uses refers to judgment, to the wrath of God. God tells one of the prophets in the Old Testament, "Take from my hand this cup of the wine of wrath, and make all the nations to whom I send you drink it" (Jeremiah 25:15).

During his ministry, Jesus uses this image to refer to his crucifixion. He tells two of his disciples, "Can you drink the cup I drink or be baptized with the baptism I am baptized with?" (Mark 10:38). And when he is praying in the garden of Gethsemane hours before his crucifixion, he asks, "Father . . . Take this cup from me. Yet not what I will, but what you will" (Mark 14:36). Just like Dumbledore, he does not want to drink the cup and asks that it might be taken away, but he ends up drinking it because he knows there is no other way for evil to be defeated.

On the cross, we see what it cost Jesus to drink this cup. Just like Dumbledore, this is the first time in Jesus' life where we see him lose his composure. Jesus certainly gets quite angry on a few occasions during his ministry, such as when he drives the money changers out of the temple; and he also breaks down in tears a number of times, such as when his friend Lazarus dies. But on the cross, Jesus is shrieking. He is in agony. He cries out in a sense of abandonment, "My God, my God, why have you forsaken me?" (Mark 15:34). And the record of his death says, "With a loud voice, he breathed his last" (Mark 15:37).

We might initially think, "Of course he is shrieking—he is being tortured to death!" But this was actually a very unusual way for a crucifixion to end. As one scholar puts it, "Most people who were crucified grew weaker and weaker and gradually and quietly expired."[206] But that is not what happens with Jesus. Something else is going on here, and the Roman centurion overseeing the execution (who certainly would have witnessed many other crucifixions) recognizes this as well: "And when the centurion, who stood there in front of Jesus, saw how he died, he said, 'Surely this man was the Son of God!'" (Mark 15:39).

The difference with Jesus' crucifixion is that he is not just experiencing the physical torture of scourging (severe whipping), beatings, a crown of thorns on his head, nails piercing his hands and feet, intense dehydration, and increasing suffocation; he is experiencing the even greater anguish of being cut off from a sense of the love of his Father with whom he had always known intimate fellowship. As the theologian Jonathan Edwards writes, "The sufferings which Christ endured in his body on the cross . . . were yet the least part of his last sufferings."[207] Or to put it in Dumbledore's words as he enters the cave, "There are much more terrible things than physical injury."[208]

There is certainly mystery here. How is it that Jesus, the embodiment of God, can be forsaken by God? Or to use the traditional Christian categories, how can two members of the Trinity be separated from each other? These are not easy questions to answer, but they do tell us something about the love of God. The love of God is such that it will go to any length—come hell or high water (in one sense quite literally)—to rescue the world.[209] It is on the cross that we see "how wide and long and high and deep is the love of Christ" (Ephesians 3:18).

But why does Jesus have to suffer this way? Why is he forsaken by God? The answer is that Jesus is suffering in the place of humanity. The apostle Paul writes, "God made him who had no sin to be sin for us, so that in him we might become the righteousness of God" (2 Corinthians 5:21). Paul is talking about Jesus here, and it is striking that he does not just say that Jesus received the *penalty* for sin (though that is certainly true as well); he says that Jesus *became sin*. And as such, Jesus was treated the way sin is treated—with judgment and exile from God, just as Adam and Eve were exiled from the garden of Eden. On the cross, Jesus was treated as if he had committed all the crimes of those he was suffering for.

And part of judgment is living with the consequences of sin. This was unpacked more in chapter 13 on Voldemort, but the Bible teaches that sin is its own punishment. The judgment of God is that he gives people over to their sin and worship of idols, a process that ends in the "second death" since these idols are lifeless and therefore cannot give life but rather take it from us. This is why Dumbledore is in agony when he drinks the emerald potion—he is being forced to relive his worst memory in vivid detail and feel the regret and guilt of it all over again. He is being forced to face the consequences of his sins with heightened intensity. And that causes him, an otherwise very composed man, to unravel.

But Jesus' agony on the cross is not just reliving a single person's worst sins—he is reliving all the sins of the whole world and experiencing the consequences as if he himself did them (1 John 2:2). Millions of atrocities throughout human history coming together in a single moment and being judged in a single person. An unfathomable weight that causes Jesus—though he stays the course—to unravel. Jesus became sin on the cross.

Dumbledore drank the potion in its entirety—twelve gobletfuls, which in the Bible is a number of completion. But Jesus drank the cup of God's wrath in its entirety for all those who trust in him. This is partly why he said, "It is finished," just before he died (John 19:30). He had completed the mission he was given by God, an essential component of which was completely exhausting the curse of sin. And therefore, though Jesus' suffering on the cross is mysterious in many ways, Dumbledore's agony as he drinks Voldemort's potion is an echo of what Jesus' agony must have been like.

Quotes from Dumbledore show up a lot in this book. There is a reason for that—the man has almost unparalleled wisdom. He is compassionate yet courageous, gentle yet firm, patient yet unrelenting, brilliant yet humble. There is much to admire. But it is in the cave that we see the full gamut of his wisdom and powers: detecting Voldemort's secret, overcoming his protective enchantments, draining his sinister potion, and still managing to conjure a fiery lasso to ward off the Inferi despite his significantly weakened state. He goes where no one else can go and does what no one else can do.

That is what the gospel is all about. At the end of the book of Isaiah, while the Israelites are in exile in Babylon because of their sin, God says,

> See, I have taken out of your hand
>   the cup that made you stagger;
> from that cup, the goblet of my wrath,
>   you will never drink again. (Isaiah 51:22)

The exile will end. The goblet of wrath will never be drunk again. Judgment will be over. The reason? Because of the servant of the Lord:

> He was pierced for our transgressions,
>   he was crushed for our iniquities;
> the punishment that brought us peace was on him,
>   and by his wounds we are healed. (Isaiah 53:5)

The New Testament teaches that the servant here is Jesus. This is the good news. For those who believe in Jesus, the consequences of their sins have fallen on him. This invitation to believe is for anyone and everyone—"for you and your children and for all who are far off" (Acts 2:39). Forgiveness of sins. The past washed away. A fresh start. All because of Jesus, who has gone where no one else could go and done what no one else could do.

20

The Forest

It was not, after all, so easy to die.[210]

THE MOST POIGNANT CHAPTER in the Harry Potter series for me has always been chapter 34 of the seventh book: "The Forest Again." It is in this chapter that we see how the story's hero, Harry, most fully takes on the role of the Christian story's hero, Jesus Christ. To be sure, there are many characters in Harry Potter—Lily, Fawkes, the Marauders, and Dumbledore, to name a few—who echo the story of Jesus, as other chapters have highlighted. But what is unique to this chapter is that we get inside Harry's head as he takes the long walk to his own death.

This is, of course, because the entire series is written from Harry's point of view, and therefore he is the only character whose thoughts and feelings we have access to.[211] Because of this, "The Forest Again" has striking similarities to the passage in the Bible where we overhear the thoughts and feelings of Jesus just as he is about to march to his own death: the story of Jesus praying in the garden of Gethsemane. Jesus knows that his death is necessary for God's mission to go forward, but he is struggling with what he must do, and his spirit is crushed. It is a quite shocking account to record, given that it was written by Jesus' followers who celebrated him as their hero. But the power of the story is that it shows in graphic detail what it cost Jesus to give his life for us.

"The Forest Again" is Harry's Gethsemane experience. I have never come across another account in literature like this chapter where the reader is given such a vivid portrayal of what is going on inside of the person who marches to their own death when they know they have the choice to walk away. Certainly many other stories have characters who sacrifice themselves for others the way Jesus did. Aslan walking to his death at the hands of the White Witch in *The Lion, the Witch, and the Wardrobe* is one well-known example. But like many other stories, the reader does not get inside the head of Aslan to know what it was like for him to do this—that is not the purpose of the story, nor is it written from Aslan's perspective. "The Forest Again" is unique, and the rest of this chapter will unpack how similar this account of Harry's affliction is to Jesus' affliction in the garden of Gethsemane.

One of Harry's greatest strengths has always been his bravery. By the time we get to the seventh book, he has faced Quirrell, Acromantulas, the Basilisk, hundreds of dementors, the three tasks of the Triwizard Tournament, Death Eaters, Inferi, and Voldemort on five different occasions, but we never get the sense that he has been all that afraid. In fact, Harry himself says so after looking at Snape's memories in the Pensieve: even though he had come to the brink of death a number of times, the heat of the moment had always distracted him from his fear of death.[212] Furthermore, when Harry and Lupin are discussing the fact that Harry sees a dementor when he encounters a boggart, Lupin responds, "Well, well . . . I'm impressed. . . . That suggests that what you fear most of all is—fear. Very wise, Harry."[213]

Harry's greatest fear is to be afraid, and up until this point, he has mostly avoided fear's paralyzing grip. But now there is no way around it. No heat of the moment to distract him. No swift end. Fear must be allowed to permeate his mind and body. Upon learning that he must die, terror drives him to the floor, and he tries to come to terms with what he must do. He considers his parents' deaths and how much easier it would have been to die quickly; his slow trudge into the forest would be far more daunting.[214]

In the garden of Gethsemane, Jesus has a similar fear. He awaits the cold-blooded walk to his own death, which would encompass scourging and beatings before the slow agony of Roman crucifixion (John 12:33). And the physiological effects of this fear are described in vivid detail. For Harry, these effects become more pronounced as he walks from Dumbledore's office to the Forbidden Forest: what begins as an escalating heart rate and quivering hands becomes uncontrollable trembling and frantic heart pulsations by the time he reaches Voldemort in the heart of the forest.[215]

For Jesus, the physiological effects are even more severe: "And being in anguish, he prayed more earnestly, and his sweat was like drops of blood falling to the ground" (Luke 22:44). Sweating blood is a very rare phenomenon that has only been observed among humans awaiting execution or being placed in a situation in which they could die. Imagine how fast your heart must be pounding and how anxious you must be in order for your body to sweat blood.

Both Jesus and Harry also have to face their deaths alone. Jesus' disciples "deserted him and fled" while he was in the garden of Gethsemane—the final evidence that the heart of his mission was misunderstood by those closest to him and that he would have to go it alone (Matthew 26:56). And while Harry's friends were still fighting for him, they would not be able to understand what he had to do, so he could not tell them—not even Ron and Hermione. Those two had been with him through thick and thin since the beginning, but "this was a journey they could not take together."[216]

Furthermore, both ordeals happen at night. Jesus draws significance from this when he says to those who come to arrest him, "But this is your hour—when darkness reigns" (Luke 22:53). In other words, it is not just dark outside; it is an hour in which evil is mounting its full assault on Jesus. Likewise, Harry must march straight into the heart of the Forbidden Forest, where it is darkest and densest and where all of Voldemort's sinister supporters have gathered.

Understandably, both Jesus and Harry would desperately like to avoid their cold-blooded walks to death. Harry wears his Invisibility Cloak as he descends from Dumbledore's office to the entrance hall to avoid being detected. But when he walks by Ginny out on the castle grounds, it takes all of his self-control to not rip off the Cloak and let her know that he was there so that he could be stopped and protected.[217] And Jesus, for his part, prays three times that he might be spared death: "My Father, if it is possible, may this cup be taken from me. Yet not as I will, but as you will" (Matthew 26:39).

As the darkness deepens and their anguish intensifies, however, both Jesus and Harry are given comfort by the ones who sent them on their missions. Harry learns from Dumbledore (through Snape's memories) that he must die in order to defeat Voldemort; Dumbledore had been the mastermind of the plan all along and knew how it had to end. But Dumbledore also knew that Harry would need strength as he faced death, so he gave him a Snitch that could only be opened "at the close"—that is, just as Harry's life was coming to a close.[218] At the end of the match, as it were.

When Harry opens the Snitch, he finds the Resurrection Stone that had been cracked in half, and James, Sirius, Lupin, and Lily appear in ghostlike bodies to comfort him. They speak consolingly to him and even walk with him through the forest to shield him like a Patronus from the dementors gliding before him.[219] Likewise, while Jesus prayed in the garden of Gethsemane, "an angel from heaven appeared to him and strengthened him" (Luke 22:43). His Father, the mastermind of his mission, sent him a comforting presence to steel his resolve as the darkness of Calvary loomed ever closer.

And though it is a struggle, both Jesus and Harry make the decision to go forward with their missions and give themselves over to death. In Harry's case, after Lily, James, Sirius, and Lupin appear just outside the forest, he knows that it is time, and he begins the trek into the heart of the forest.[220] In the case of Jesus, he prays, "My Father, if it is not possible for this cup to be taken away unless I drink it, may your will be done" (Matthew 26:42). And he tells those who come to arrest him, "Do what you came for" (Matthew 26:50).

This climaxes in Jesus' crucifixion, where the heart of his agony is a sense of betrayal at the hands of the one who sent him to die: "My God, my God, why have you forsaken me?" (Matthew 27:45). But Harry also experiences shocking betrayal as he walks into the forest: he had just witnessed Dumbledore telling Snape over a year prior that the plan all along was that Harry would have to die.[221] He had always thought that Dumbledore loved him and was trying to protect him—was this love?

The most admirable element in all of this is that both Jesus and Harry could have walked away at any time. When Jesus is arrested and his disciples try to defend him, he says, "Do you think I cannot call on my Father, and he will at once put at my disposal more than twelve legions of angels?" (Matthew 26:53). At any point during the sham trials or mocking or beatings or the hours he hung on the cross, Jesus could have called in reinforcements and been saved. He could have climbed out of the abyss at any time. But he did not—he endured. Harry, likewise, could have run from it all. He could have Apparated to somewhere far away, like Aberforth told him to do. It was a long walk from Dumbledore's office to the heart of the Forbidden Forest, with many opportunities to turn back. But he kept walking. Each step would have required extraordinary courage and iron determination as every fiber of his being begged him to turn back.

Ultimately, the journeys of both Jesus and Harry end with death (though it is more complicated in Harry's case). It is very fitting, then, that after Harry gets struck with the Killing Curse, he winds up in what looks like King's Cross Station. The name of the train station originates from a monument to King George IV, but as Rowling says, it is an "evocative and symbolic name."[222]

When Jesus came, he spoke and acted as if he was a king—the Messiah—and he was crucified on a cross. Moreover, he was given a crown of thorns, and the inscription above his cross read, "The King of the Jews," indicating that this was the crime for which he was being crucified (Matthew 27:37). The irony of it all, though, is that all four Gospels portray this as the moment when Jesus actually became king—the moment when he conquered the kingdoms of darkness and was enthroned over every other ruler. Jesus is a different kind of king: one who delivers his people from the powers of darkness by taking its full force upon himself; one who reigns with the power of self-giving love; one who is enthroned on a cross. This is what it means to be the Messiah. Therefore, after Harry has so closely mirrored the suffering of Jesus in giving his life to take Voldemort's death-curse square in the chest, consequently freeing his friends from the power of Voldemort's curses, King's Cross Station is a perfect destination for him.

Fundamentally, this is who the God of the Bible is—the king who is enthroned on a cross. This is how God has made himself known:

> The Word became flesh and made his dwelling among us. We have seen his glory, the glory of the one and only Son, who came from the Father, full of grace and truth. . . . No one has ever seen God, but the one and only Son, who is himself God and is in closest relationship with the Father, has made him known. (John 1:14, 18)

People have lots of ideas about who God is and what he is like. Some say that he is distant and indifferent, others that he is angry and malevolent, perhaps others that he is a tolerant pushover, or else that he is equally knowable in every aspect of our world. The God of the Bible is none of those: He is the God who reveals what he is like when he is crucified. He is the God who marches to his own death. He is the God of the King's Cross.

Conclusion

Resurrection

A red-gold glow burst suddenly across the enchanted sky above.

—In the Great Hall just before Voldemort dies[223]

DEATH LEADS TO TEARS and sorrow; that is what happens when someone we know and love dies. When Hagrid, McGonagall, Ron, Hermione, Ginny, and all the rest who fought Voldemort see Harry's limp body at the front of the procession, they begin to weep, thinking him dead. And not just weep—there is bitterness and despair, as is evident when Professor McGonagall screams, "NO!"[224] The Chosen One, the Boy Who Lived, the one they hoped would defeat Lord Voldemort had been killed. Expectations and hopes were dashed. Voldemort, the one who had caused so much pain and destruction and loss—one need only look in the Great Hall to see the dead bodies of Fred, Tonks, Lupin, and fifty others—appeared to have won. Thus the bitter tears.

But death does not have the last word in Harry Potter. Resurrection does. Harry returns to his body lying on the ground in the Forbidden Forest. And what builds the tension in this final chapter is that the reader knows Harry is alive, but none of the characters in the story know this except for Narcissa Malfoy. In the tumult of the centaurs, thestrals, house-elves, and other witches and wizards arriving to fight the Death Eaters, Harry is able to cover himself with his Invisibility Cloak. Then he reveals to everyone in the Great Hall that he is alive, and Voldemort is vanquished once and for all.

The result is utter pandemonium. Shouts and cheers of joy resound all around Harry as Ron, Hermione, Ginny, Neville, Luna, the Weasleys, the Hogwarts teachers, and the hundreds of others who fought Voldemort press in around Harry, trying to touch any part of him—their victor and their hero.[225] The sun has risen and the darkness has scattered. Light is shining into the Great Hall once again. Friends are reunited and feasting and laughing together. And the head of the snake Nagini has been cut off. Good has triumphed because Harry has been raised from the dead.

Of course, Jesus himself is the archetypal picture of resurrection. This is the foundation upon which the Christian faith stands or falls: "If Christ has not been raised, your faith is futile; you are still in your sins" (1 Corinthians 15:17). It all hinges on this. Most people find the prospect of a dead person being resurrected incredulous, with good reason. Those in Jesus' day thought likewise. Many books have analyzed the historical likelihood of Jesus' resurrection, which cannot be discussed here. My point, instead, is that resurrection plays the same role in both stories—the role of the happy ending. Of good news. Of gospel.

The overlap in the events leading up to resurrection in the two stories is remarkable. Just like Harry's, Jesus' death caused great grief. There were bitter tears of despair at his tomb. Jesus was believed to be the Messiah, the Chosen One who would deliver Israel from evil; as his disciples said, "He was a prophet, powerful in word and deed before God and all the people. The chief priests and our rulers handed him over to be sentenced to death, and they crucified him; but we had hoped that he was the one who was going to redeem Israel" (Luke 24:19–21). Because Jesus had been killed, all hopes that he could be the Messiah were dashed.

This is why the dominant mood that runs through the resurrection stories is one of joy and amazement: the followers of Jesus could not believe what happened. Jesus' resurrection changed everything. All four Gospels emphasize that Jesus rose on the *first* day of the week, and, echoing the creation story in Genesis 1, it means that something new is coming into being. It all starts in a garden again (John 20:15), but this time there is no snake. The head of the snake has been crushed (see Genesis 3:15). A new day has come and light is shining on a world in darkness (Ephesians 5:14).

But there is an even deeper connection between Harry's resurrection and Jesus' resurrection. When Harry sees the inscription on his parents' tombstone in Godric's Hollow that speaks of the defeat of death, he first thinks that this is a Death Eater idea. But Hermione points out that this is a different way of defeating death: it means "living beyond death. Living after death."[226]

"But they were not living, thought Harry: They were gone."[227] Harry saw his parents when his wand linked with Voldemort's in the Little Hangleton graveyard, producing the *Priori Incantatem* effect, and he would see them again in the Forbidden Forest when he rubbed the Resurrection Stone in his hands just before he died. But he knows this is not what it means to defeat death, which is why he begins to cry. His parents' bodies are rotting away underneath their tombstone; they cannot be with him. Living beyond death is not the same as destroying it.

This is what makes Harry's resurrection different. He does not take the train "On" as Dumbledore suggests he can do.[228] He does not become a ghost. He does not live on in the ways that Dumbledore, his parents, Sirius, and Lupin did. He comes back to earth in his body. This is what it means to defeat death, and in this way he embodies the true Christian hope.

When Jesus rose from the dead, he was also embodied; it was his own body, though transformed in some ways. And the apostle Paul says that because Jesus has been raised, all those who believe in him will be raised from the dead as well:

> But Christ has indeed been raised from the dead, the firstfruits of those who have fallen asleep. For since death came through a man, the resurrection of the dead comes also through a man. For as in Adam all die, so in Christ all will be made alive. But each in turn: Christ, the

firstfruits; then, when he comes, those who belong to him.
(1 Corinthians 15:20–23)

This is the ultimate Christian hope—not a spiritual existence but a material, bodily one. And Paul goes even further than that. He says that because Jesus has been raised from the dead, not only will all those who believe in him be raised, all of creation will likewise experience a resurrection:

> I consider that our present sufferings are not worth comparing with the glory that will be revealed in us. For the creation waits in eager expectation for the children of God to be revealed. For the creation was subjected to frustration, not by its own choice, but by the will of the one who subjected it, in hope that the creation itself will be liberated from its bondage to decay and brought into the freedom and glory of the children of God. We know that the whole creation has been groaning as in the pains of childbirth right up to the present time. (Romans 8:18–22)

When the children of God are raised from the dead, the whole creation will join in their freedom from corruption and decay. This is what it means in Christianity for death to be defeated. Not an ethereal life somewhere else. Not a consolation prize for all that death took from us on earth. Rather, it is nothing short of a new heaven and a new earth—a restored world in which all things are made new:

> Then I saw "a new heaven and a new earth," for the first heaven and the first earth had passed away. . . . Then the angel showed me the river of the water of life, as clear as crystal, flowing from the throne of God and of the Lamb down the middle of the great street of the city. On each side of the river stood the tree of life, bearing twelve crops of fruit, yielding its fruit every month. And the leaves of the tree are for the healing of the nations. (Revelation 21:1; 22:1–2)

This hope is entirely unique among the other world religions and worldviews. Luc Ferry, a French philosopher who is not himself a

Christian, says, "The Christian response to mortality, for believers at least, is without question the most 'effective' of all responses: it would seem to be the only version of salvation that enables us not only to transcend the fear of death, but also to beat death itself."[229]

Many religions hold out the hope of life after death in the form of eternal bliss or paradise, but only Christianity teaches that death will not just be transcended but destroyed—even reversed. No religion before Christianity had ever said something like this, and no one since has had the audacity to make this claim.[230] Ferry goes so far as to even call the Christian story "tempting" and "seductive."[231] Who would not want to live in a renewed world where evil is gone for good and all that is broken is healed?

I think of my own regrets and the foolish decisions I wish I had not made—a pang that I believe many can resonate with. Other religions offer the consolation of peace and rest in the afterlife. Christianity offers a restoration of all that was lost and then some. If you were inventing a form of salvation, you could not come up with something better than this, which is why Tolkien called the gospel the greatest of all fairy tales. Ferry would say that it is too good to be true, but this is what Christianity teaches will happen, and Harry's resurrection is a resounding echo of it.

Resurrection is not the end, though—it is a new beginning. The *final* new beginning. In the Epilogue we get a glimpse of what life is like post-Voldemort, and the last line encapsulates it perfectly: "The scar had not pained Harry for nineteen years. All was well."[232] The scar remains. Just like Harry, Jesus keeps his scars after his resurrection (John 20:27). But the pain is gone. And what *was* a cause of pain and death—nails driven into his hands and feet and a spear piercing his side—becomes a sign of victory. The scars become a sign that death has been defeated. The same is true of Harry's scar: it marks him as the Boy Who Lived, the one who finally defeated Voldemort.

And there is no chance of Voldemort's return this time. That is part of what it means that "all was well." There is no potential for evil to reenter this world. The final vision of the Bible closes similarly:

No longer will there be any curse. The throne of God and
of the Lamb will be in the city, and his servants will serve
him. They will see his face, and his name will be on their
foreheads. There will be no more night. They will not
need the light of a lamp or the light of the sun, for the
Lord God will give them light. And they will reign for
ever and ever. (Revelation 22:3–5)

This is the biblical vision of salvation: resurrected bodies in a resurrected world worshiping and reigning with a resurrected Lord.
And again, this is not the end; it is a new beginning. Evil and darkness have been quarantined forever from this new world. And it
opens up a whole host of new possibilities and adventures to be explored: worshiping and reigning forever and ever. Or as C. S. Lewis
put it at the end of his Chronicles of Narnia series, "All their life
in this world and all their adventures in Narnia had only been the
cover and the title page: now at last they were beginning Chapter
One of the Great Story which no one on earth has read: which goes
on for ever: in which every chapter is better than the one before."[233]

J. R. R. Tolkien closes his essay "On Fairy-Stories" like this:

But in God's kingdom the presence of the greatest does
not depress the small. . . . Story, fantasy, still go on, and
should go on. The [gospel] has not abrogated legends; it
has hallowed them, especially the "happy ending." The
Christian has still to work, with mind as well as body,
to suffer, hope, and die; but he may now perceive that
all his bents and faculties have a purpose, which can be
redeemed. So great is the bounty with which he has been
treated that he may now, perhaps, fairly dare to guess
that in Fantasy he may actually assist in the effoliation[234]
and multiple enrichment of creation. All tales may come
true; and yet, at the last, redeemed, they may be as like
and as unlike the forms that we give them as Man, finally redeemed, will be like and unlike the fallen that we
know.[235]

The gospel is the greatest of fairy tales, and it has come true. But
Tolkien says that does not do away with other fairy tales; rather, it
hallows or dignifies them. "All tales may come true"—this is why

Harry Potter has even more significance for the Christian. It is not just a magnificent story; it is part of what Tolkien calls the enrichment of creation. It is part of the new creation that began with Jesus' resurrection. And according to Christian teaching, it will, in a sense, come true and find its final fulfillment and redemption in the world to come.

This is why the apostle Paul closes his teaching on the resurrection in 1 Corinthians 15 like this: "Therefore, my dear brothers and sisters, stand firm. Let nothing move you. Always give yourselves fully to the work of the Lord, because you know that your labor in the Lord is not in vain" (15:58). Because of Jesus' resurrection—because there is a future for our world—the work we do now is not in vain. As Tolkien says, there are basic tasks we all must do: we must love, work, suffer, hope, and die, among many other things. But the resurrection of Jesus gives meaning and purpose to all of them. And therefore, Harry Potter, with its resurrection new beginning, not only gives a vision of the resurrection to come, it is in some mysterious way a part of that resurrection. And one day, it may very well come true.

Endnotes

1. It is unknown who first said this, but it is often attributed to Gregory the Great in the sixth century AD.

2. "500 Million Harry Potter Books."

3. Tolkien, "On Fairy-Stories," 57–58.

4. Tolkien, "On Fairy-Stories," 60–68.

5. Tolkien, "On Fairy-Stories," 68–69.

6. Tolkien, "On Fairy-Stories," 72.

7. They are Matthew 6:21 and 1 Corinthians 15:26, and they appear on tombstones in Godric's Hollow in the seventh book. Rowling, *Deathly Hallows*, 325, 328.

8. Petre, "'Christianity Inspired Harry Potter.'"

9. Tolkien, "On Fairy-Stories," 72.

10. Rowling, *Sorcerer's Stone*, 17.

11. Rowling, *Sorcerer's Stone*, 10.

12. Tolkien, "On Fairy-Stories," 72.

13. Rowling, *Order of the Phoenix*, 841.

14. Rowling, *Half-Blood Prince*, 510.

15. Rowling, *Sorcerer's Stone*, 5.

16. Rowling, *Sorcerer's Stone*, 50.

17. Rowling, *Half-Blood Prince*, 188.

18. Rowling, *Goblet of Fire*, 151.

19. Rowling, *Order of the Phoenix*, 484.

20. Tolkien, "On Fairy-Stories," 66–67.

21. Rowling, *Sorcerer's Stone*, 213.

22. Rowling, *Sorcerer's Stone*, 207.

23. Rowling, *Sorcerer's Stone*, 213.

24. Rowling, *Deathly Hallows*, 719.

25. Rowling, *Deathly Hallows*, 325.

26. Wallace, "This Is Water."

27. Rowling, *Sorcerer's Stone*, 213.

28. See chapter 15 for more on this. The Bible affirms the reality of evil as both something that humans participate in and as something that is supernatural and larger than human evil.

29. Rowling, *Sorcerer's Stone*, 213.

30. Rowling, *Chamber of Secrets*, 62.

31. Rowling, *Chamber of Secrets*, 115–16.

32. Rowling, *Deathly Hallows*, 10–11.

33. Rowling, *Chamber of Secrets*, 178.

34. Rowling, *Deathly Hallows*, 242.

35. Rowling, *Half-Blood Prince*, 207–8.

36. Rowling, *Goblet of Fire*, 708.

37. Tisby, *Color of Compromise*, 20–21.

38. This insight came from Wright, "Undermining Racism."

39. Rowling, *Deathly Hallows*, 745.

40. Rowling, *Goblet of Fire*, 708.

41. Rowling, *Half-Blood Prince*, 497.

42. Rowling, *Half-Blood Prince*, 497–98.

43. Rowling, *Half-Blood Prince*, 502.

44. According to the footnotes in the NIV Bible, this is "an Aramaic word of contempt."

45. Rowling, *Deathly Hallows*, 103.

46. Rowling, *Deathly Hallows*, 479.

47. See chapter 15 for more on this.

48. Rowling, *Order of the Phoenix*, 841.

49. Wright, *After You Believe*, 116.

50. Rowling, *Deathly Hallows*, 409–10.

51. Rowling, *Sorcerer's Stone*, 11.

52. Rowling, *Goblet of Fire*, 679.

53. Rowling, *Goblet of Fire*, 525.

54. Rowling, *Deathly Hallows*, 718.

55. Rowling, *Deathly Hallows*, 720.

56. Rowling, *Deathly Hallows*, 716.

57. Rowling, *Deathly Hallows*, 720.

58. Rowling, *Deathly Hallows*, 711, 721.

59. Rowling, *Deathly Hallows*, 718.

60. Rowling, *Deathly Hallows*, 746.

61. Lewis, *Four Loves*, 73.

62. Rowling, *Sorcerer's Stone*, 179.

63. Rowling, *Half-Blood Prince*, 78.

64. These characteristics of friendship were taken from Keller and Keller, *Meaning of Marriage*, 121.

65. Rowling, *Half-Blood Prince*, 430.

66. Rowling, *Half-Blood Prince*, 277.

67. Rowling, *Half-Blood Prince*, 99.

68. Rowling, *Half-Blood Prince*, 651.

69. Rowling, *Deathly Hallows*, 99.

70. Keller and Keller, *Meaning of Marriage*, 101.

71. William Penn, *More Fruits of Solitude*, quoted in Rowling, *Deathly Hallows*, xvii.

72. Cuarón, *Prisoner of Azkaban.*

73. Rowling, *Sorcerer's Stone*, 299.

74. Rowling, *Order of the Phoenix*, 836.

75. Rowling, *Deathly Hallows*, 709.

76. Rowling, *Half-Blood Prince*, 444.

77. Other spells, it seems, are broken when the one who cast them dies, such as when Dumbledore's Freezing Charm over Harry breaks after he dies in the sixth book.

78. Rowling, *Order of the Phoenix*, 843.

79. This insight came from Wright, *Day the Revolution Began*, 169–70.

80. Rowling, *Deathly Hallows*, 687.

81. Rowling, *Order of the Phoenix*, 496.

82. Rowling, *Sorcerer's Stone*, 302.

83. Rowling, *Prisoner of Azkaban*, 393.

84. Rowling, *Deathly Hallows*, 72.

85. Rowling, *Deathly Hallows*, 362.

86. Rowling, *Deathly Hallows*, 483.

87. Rowling, *Deathly Hallows*, 685.

88. Rowling, *Deathly Hallows*, 720.

89. The Greek word here can mean both "temptation" and "trial."

90. This insight came from Keller, *Counterfeit Gods*, 18.

91. Rowling, *Chamber of Secrets*, 338.

92. Rowling, *Chamber of Secrets*, 14.

93. Rowling, *Order of the Phoenix*, 386.

94. Rowling, *Deathly Hallows*, 481.

95. Taylor, *Secular Age*, 484.

96. Keller, *Preaching*, 144.

97. Rowling, *Goblet of Fire*, 664.

98. "Christ Figure."

99. Rowling, *Chamber of Secrets*, 207.

100. Rowling, *Chamber of Secrets*, 332.

101. Rowling, *Chamber of Secrets*, 321.

102. Rowling, *Chamber of Secrets*, 315.

103. Rowling, *Goblet of Fire*, 664.

104. Rowling, *Order of the Phoenix*, 807

105. Rowling, *Half-Blood Prince*, 614–15.

106. Brown, "Brené Brown on Empathy," RSA.

107. Keller and Keller, *Songs of Jesus*, viii.

108. Rowling, *Half-Blood Prince*, 615.

109. Rowling, *Prisoner of Azkaban*, 355.

110. Rowling, *Prisoner of Azkaban*, 354–55.

111. Rowling, *Prisoner of Azkaban*, 354.

112. Stott, *Cross of Christ*, 327.

113. Rowling, *Chamber of Secrets*, 314.

114. Keller, *Walking with God*, 53.

115. Rowling, *Sorcerer's Stone*, 297.

116. Rowling, *Deathly Hallows*, 722.

117. Rowling, *Prisoner of Azkaban*, 247.

118. Rowling, *Prisoner of Azkaban*, 247.

119. Rowling, *Order of the Phoenix*, 814.

120. Rowling, *Half-Blood Prince*, 497.

121. Rowling, *Deathly Hallows*, 707, 709.

122. Rowling, *Deathly Hallows*, 722.

123. Rowling, *Half-Blood Prince*, 445–46.

124. Rowling, *Deathly Hallows*, 741.

125. See chapter 5 for more on how remorse has the power to put the soul back together.

126. Rowling, *Goblet of Fire*, 607.

127. Volf, *Exclusion and Embrace*, 290–96.

128. Rowling, *Deathly Hallows*, 679.

129. Rowling, *Order of the Phoenix*, 591–92.

130. Rowling, *Deathly Hallows*, 676.

131. Rowling, *Half-Blood Prince*, 262.

132. Rowling, *Deathly Hallows*, 678.

133. Rowling, *Deathly Hallows*, 679.

134. Rowling, *Deathly Hallows*, 685.

135. This insight into Romans 8 came from Wright, *Day the Revolution Began*, 371–72.

136. Rowling, *Sorcerer's Stone*, 297.

137. HarryPotterAdmirer, "JK Rowling and Daniel Radcliffe."

138. Rowling, *Order of the Phoenix*, 302.

139. Yates, *Order of the Phoenix*.

140. Rowling, *Order of the Phoenix*, 474–75.

141. Solzhenitsyn, *Gulag Archipelago*, 615.

142. Wright, *Surprised by Hope*, 87.

143. Rowling, *Half-Blood Prince*, 645.

144. Rowling, *Half-Blood Prince*, 177.

145. Rowling, *Half-Blood Prince*, 560.

146. Rowling, *Goblet of Fire*, 527.

147. Rowling, *Goblet of Fire*, 723.

148. King, *Strength to Love*, 37.

149. Rowling, *Chamber of Secrets*, 334.

150. Rowling, *Sorcerer's Stone*, 287.

151. Rowling, *Goblet of Fire*, 724.

152. Rowling, *Chamber of Secrets*, 333.

153. Rowling, *Order of the Phoenix*, 477.

154. Rowling, *Order of the Phoenix*, 94.

155. Rowling, *Sorcerer's Stone*, 306.

156. Ju, "Courage Is the Most Important Virtue."

157. Rowling, *Deathly Hallows*, 680.

158. Rowling, *Deathly Hallows*, 678.

159. Rowling, *Deathly Hallows*, 687.

160. Rowling, *Deathly Hallows*, 687.

161. Rowling, *Deathly Hallows*, 758.

162. Perry, *Gay Girl, Good God*, 174–75.

163. Rowling, *Deathly Hallows*, 749.

164. Brand and Yancey, *Gift of Pain*, 12.

165. Gray, *Straw Dogs*, 142.

166. Haidt, *Happiness Hypothesis*, 136.

167. Haidt, *Happiness Hypothesis*, 138.

168. Rowling, *Order of the Phoenix*, 823.

169. Rowling, *Order of the Phoenix*, 816.

170. Rowling, *Deathly Hallows*, 478.

171. Rowling, *Order of the Phoenix*, 841.

172. Rowling, *Half-Blood Prince*, 509.

173. Rowling, *Order of the Phoenix*, 650.

174. Rowling, *Half-Blood Prince*, 510–11.

175. Rowling, *Deathly Hallows*, 720.

176. Rowling, *Half-Blood Prince*, 186.

177. Potok, *Chosen*, 284, 286.

178. Rowling, *Deathly Hallows*, 16–20.

179. Keller, *Walking with God*, 9.

180. Rowling, *Half-Blood Prince*, 632.

181. HarryPotterAdmirer, "JK Rowling and Steve Kloves."

182. Petre, "J. K. Rowling: 'Christianity Inspired Harry Potter.'" Rowling says, concerning this quotation and Matthew 6:21, which is engraved on the tombstone of Dumbledore's mother and sister, "They sum up, they almost epitomise, the whole series."

183. Rowling, *Deathly Hallows*, 328.

184. Rowling, *Deathly Hallows*, 714, 720.

185. Poe, "The Raven."

186. Becker, *Denial of Death*, xvii.

187. Rowling, *Goblet of Fire*, 653.

188. Rowling, *Half-Blood Prince*, 502.

189. Rowling, *Half-Blood Prince*, 502.

190. Rowling, *Half-Blood Prince*, 363.

191. Rowling, *Deathly Hallows*, 717.

192. Rowling, *Deathly Hallows*, 434–35.

193. Rowling, *Deathly Hallows*, 500.

194. Rowling, *Deathly Hallows*, 720.

195. Herbert, "Time."

196. Rowling, *Half-Blood Prince*, 580.

197. HarryPotterAdmirer, "JK Rowling and Daniel Radcliffe."

198. Rowling, *Half-Blood Prince*, 559.

199. Rowling, *Half-Blood Prince*, 571.

200. Rowling, *Half-Blood Prince*, 572.

201. Rowling, *Half-Blood Prince*, 572.

202. Rowling, *Half-Blood Prince*, 573.

203. Rowling, *Half-Blood Prince*, 573.

204. Rowling, *Deathly Hallows*, 568.

205. Rowling, *Deathly Hallows*, 718.

206. Brooks, *Mark*, 262.

207. Edwards, "Christ's Agony," 869.

208. Rowling, *Half-Blood Prince*, 559.

209. This insight came from Wright, *Day the Revolution Began*, 292–94.

210. Rowling, *Deathly Hallows*, 697.

211. There are a few chapters that are not written from Harry's perspective: "The Boy Who Lived" in *Harry Potter and the Sorcerer's Stone*; "The Riddle House" in *Harry Potter and the Goblet of Fire*; "The Other Minister" and "Spinner's End" in *Harry Potter and the Half-Blood Prince*; and "The Dark Lord Ascending" in *Harry Potter and the Deathly Hallows*.

212. Rowling, *Deathly Hallows*, 692.

213. Rowling, *Prisoner of Azkaban*, 155.

214. Rowling, *Deathly Hallows*, 692.

215. Rowling, *Deathly Hallows*, 691–703.

216. Rowling, *Deathly Hallows*, 693.

217. Rowling, *Deathly Hallows*, 697.

218. Rowling, *Deathly Hallows*, 698.

219. Rowling, *Deathly Hallows*, 699–700.

220. Rowling, *Deathly Hallows*, 700.

221. Rowling, *Deathly Hallows*, 692.

222. Rowling, "Why I Chose King's Cross."

223. Rowling, *Deathly Hallows*, 743.

224. Rowling, *Deathly Hallows*, 730.

225. Rowling, *Deathly Hallows*, 744.

226. Rowling, *Deathly Hallows*, 328.

227. Rowling, *Deathly Hallows*, 328.

228. Rowling, *Deathly Hallows*, 722.

229. Ferry, *Brief History of Thought*, 90.

230. Though it is important to note that Christianity is building on the belief that many Jews had of a future resurrection (see John 11:24).

231. Ferry, *Brief History of Thought*, 85–86.

232. Rowling, *Deathly Hallows*, 759.

233. Lewis, *Last Battle*, 211.

234. This word refers to the removal of leaves from a plant.

235. Tolkien, "On Fairy-Stories," 73.

Bibliography

"500 Million Harry Potter Books Have Now Been Sold Worldwide." Wizarding World, February 1, 2018. https://www.wizardingworld.com/news/500-million-harry-potter-books-have-now-been-sold-worldwide.

Becker, Ernest. *The Denial of Death*. New York: Free Press, 1973.

Brand, Paul, and Philip Yancey. *The Gift of Pain: Why We Hurt and What We Can Do about It*. Grand Rapids: Zondervan, 1997.

Brooks, James A. *Mark*. New American Commentary. Nashville: B&H, 1991.

Brown, Brené. "Brené Brown on Empathy." RSA, December 10, 2013. https://www.thersa.org/discover/videos/rsa-shorts/2013/12/Brene-Brown-on-Empathy.

"Christ Figure." Wikipedia, acessed October 11, 2019. https://en.wikipedia.org/wiki/Christ_figure.

Cuarón, Alfonso, dir. *Harry Potter and the Prisoner of Azkaban*. London: Warner Bros., 2004. DVD.

Edwards, Jonathan. "Christ's Agony." In *The Works of Jonathan Edwards*, edited by Edward Hickman, 2:866–77. Edinburgh: Banner of Truth, 1974.

Ferry, Luc. *A Brief History of Thought: A Philosophical Guide to Living*. New York: Harper Perennial, 2011.

Gray, John. *Straw Dogs: Thoughts on Humans and Other Animals*. New York: Farrar, Straus, and Giroux, 2002.

Haidt, Jonathan. *The Happiness Hypothesis: Putting Ancient Wisdom and Philosophy to the Test of Modern Science*. New York: Basic, 2006.

HarryPotterAdmirer. "A Conversation between JK Rowling and Daniel Radcliffe." *YouTube*, September 22, 2013, 53:03. https://www.youtube.com/watch?v=7BdVHWz1DPU.

———. "A Conversation between JK Rowling and Steve Kloves." *YouTube*, November 21, 2016, 47:28. https://www.youtube.com/watch?v=LoBPOZznSvY.

Herbert, George. "Time." In *The Temple*, 186. London: Penguin Classics, 2017. First published 1633.

Ju, Anne. "Courage Is the Most Important Virtue, Says Writer and Civil Rights Activist Maya Angelou at Convocation." *Cornell Chronicle*, May 24, 2008. https://news.cornell.edu/stories/2008/05/courage-most-important-virtue-maya-angelou-tells-seniors.

Keller, Timothy. *Counterfeit Gods: The Empty Promises of Money, Sex, and Power, and the Only Hope That Matters*. New York: Penguin, 2009.

⸻. *Preaching: Communicating Faith in an Age of Skepticism*. New York: Viking, 2015.

⸻. *Walking with God through Pain and Suffering*. New York: Penguin, 2013.

Keller, Timothy, and Kathy Keller. *The Meaning of Marriage: Facing the Complexities of Commitment with the Wisdom of God*. New York: Riverhead, 2011.

⸻. *The Songs of Jesus: A Year of Daily Devotions in the Psalms*. New York: Viking, 2015.

King, Martin Luther, Jr. *Strength to Love*. New York: Harper and Row, 1963.

Lewis, C. S. *The Four Loves*. New York: HarperCollins, 2002. First published 1960 by Geoffrey Bles.

⸻. *The Last Battle*. New York: HarperCollins, 1956.

Perry, Jackie Hill. *Gay Girl, Good God*. Nashville: B&H, 2018.

Petre, Jonathan. "J. K. Rowling: 'Christianity Inspired Harry Potter.'" *The Telegraph*. October 20, 2007. https://www.telegraph.co.uk/culture/books/fictionreviews/3668658/J-K-Rowling-Christianity-inspired-Harry-Potter.html.

Poe, Edgar Allan. "The Raven." In *Edgar Allen Poe: Complete Tales and Poems*, 703. Edison, NJ: Castle Books, 2002. First published 1845 by *New York Evening Mirror*.

Potok, Chaim. *The Chosen*. New York: Random House, 1967.

Rowling, J. K. *Harry Potter and the Chamber of Secrets*. New York: Scholastic, 1998.

⸻. *Harry Potter and the Deathly Hallows*. New York: Scholastic, 2007.

⸻. *Harry Potter and the Goblet of Fire*. New York: Scholastic, 2000.

⸻. *Harry Potter and the Half-Blood Prince*. New York: Scholastic, 2005.

⸻. *Harry Potter and the Order of the Phoenix*. New York: Scholastic, 2003.

⸻. *Harry Potter and the Prisoner of Azkaban*. New York: Scholastic, 1999.

⸻. *Harry Potter and the Sorcerer's Stone*. New York: Scholastic, 1997.

⸻. "JK Rowling: Why I Chose King's Cross for Platform 9 ¾." *The Guardian*, May 20, 2015. https://www.theguardian.com/childrens-books-site/competition/2015/may/20/jk-rowling-harry-potter-kings-cross-competition.

Solzhenitsyn, Alexander. *The Gulag Archipelago, 1918–1956*. Volume 2: *An Experiment in Literary Investigation*. New York: Harper & Row, 1974.

Steinbeck, John. *East of Eden*. New York: Penguin, 2002. First published 1952 by Viking.

Stott, John. *The Cross of Christ*. Downers Grove: InterVarsity, 1986.

Taylor, Charles. *A Secular Age*. Cambridge: Harvard University Press, 2007.

Tisby, Jemar. *The Color of Compromise: The Truth about the American Church's Complicity in Racism*. Grand Rapids: Zondervan, 2019.

Tolkien, J. R. R. "On Fairy-Stories." In *Tree and Leaf*, 1–81. London: HarperCollins, 2001. First published 1964 by George Allen & Unwin.

Volf, Miroslav. *Exclusion and Embrace: A Theological Exploration of Identity, Otherness, and Reconciliation.* Nashville: Abingdon, 2019. First edition 1996.

Wallace, David Foster. "This Is Water." Farnam Street. https://fs.blog/2012/04/david-foster-wallace-this-is-water/.

Wright, N. T. *After You Believe: Why Christian Character Matters.* New York: HarperCollins, 2010.

———. *The Day the Revolution Began: Rethinking the Meaning of Jesus' Crucifixion.* New York: HarperCollins, 2016.

———. *Surprised by Hope: Rethinking Heaven, the Resurrection, and the Mission of the Church.* New York: HarperCollins, 2008.

———. "Undermining Racism." NTWrightPage, June 8, 2020. https://ntwrightpage.com/2020/06/14/undermining-racism-complete-text/.

Yates, David, dir. *Harry Potter and the Order of the Phoenix.* London: Warner Bros., 2007. DVD.

Scripture Index

OLD TESTAMENT